PRAISE FOR

TABULA RASA

"[John McPhee's] talent at turning any subject that interests him into writing that is fresh and compelling is unmatched. He is always a deep pleasure to read . . . [*Tabula Rasa*] is as close to an autobiography as we will get."　　　　　—Jim Kelly, *Air Mail*

"An insightful book by a master of literary non-fiction . . . As he explores what might have been, Mr. McPhee also proves how enjoyable it can be to spend time with such an expert storyteller."
—*The Economist*

"What do you do when your writing career lasts seven decades but you haven't said everything you once thought about saying? If you're John McPhee, you crack open your notebooks and give fans a taste of the stories you never wrote . . . *Tabula Rasa* demonstrates just how broad McPhee's 'tabula' has always been. He's like an NBA star who always has the green light to shoot."
—Rob Merrill, Associated Press

"The cogency, potency, and temperance of [John McPhee's] voice never waver . . . A gem from an exemplar of narrative nonfiction."
—*Kirkus Reviews* (starred review)

"McPhee's gift for language is on full display . . . A revealing compendium of curios from a first-rate writer."
—*Publishers Weekly*

John McPhee

TABULA RASA

John McPhee is a staff writer at *The New Yorker*. He is the author of thirty-two books, all published by Farrar, Straus and Giroux. He lives in Princeton, New Jersey.

Also by John McPhee

TABULA RASA

TABULA RASA

VOLUME 1

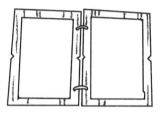

John McPhee

Picador
Farrar, Straus and Giroux
New York

Picador

120 Broadway, New York 10271

Portions of this book previously appeared, in slightly different form,
in *The New Yorker*. Portions of "Sloop to Gibraltar" previously appeared,
in slightly different form, in *Looking for a Ship*.

Tablet illustration by Meighan Cavanaugh.

Library of Congress Control Number: 2023007081

Paperback ISBN: 978-1-250-33570-8

Designed by Patrice Sheridan

1   3   5   7   9   10   8   6   4   2

For and To
Yolanda Whitman

Contents

TABULA RASA

Trujillo

By the way, did you ever write about Extremadura—and when you made that trip with Tim and Wendy did you go to Trujillo?

Dear Jenny: I didn't go there with Tim and Wendy. We drove from France straight to northern Portugal through Castilla la Vieja—Valladolid and Salamanca—and back the same way a few weeks later. Extremadura, though—just the name of it and its remoteness in the Spanish context—had some sort of romantic appeal to me from the first time I ever heard of it, which was probably when I went to Madrid and spent a couple of weeks in Jane del Amo's apartment, in 1954. I was so beguiled by Extremadura that I started writing a short story called "The Girl from Badajoz." With respect to publication, she stayed in Badajoz. But try saying "Badajoz" in castellano. It's beautiful. When you were five years old, in midsummer, we went south to north across Extremadura in our new VW microbus. It was the first time any of us had ever been there, and those were two of the hottest days of all our lives. Fahrenheit, the temperatures were in three digits. Only the oaks were cool in their insulating cork. Rubber flanges surrounded each of the many windows in the VW bus, and the cement that held the rubber flanges melted in the heat, causing the flanges to hang down from all the windows like fettuccine. We stayed in a parador in Mérida that had been a convent in the eighteenth century. Next day, the heat was just as intense, and we developed huge thirst but soon had nothing in the car to drink. Parched in Extremadura—with people like Sarah and Martha howling, panting, and mewling—we saw across the plain a hilltop town, a mile or two from the highway, and we turned to go there and quench the thirst. The roads were not much wider than the car; the national dual highways, the autovías, were still off in the future. The prospect seemed as modest as it was isolated—just another Spanish townscape distorted by heat shimmers. A sign by the portal gate said TRUJILLO. We drove to it, and into it, and up through its helical streets, and finally into its central plaza. There—suddenly and surprisingly towering over us—was a much larger than life equestrian statue of Francisco Pizarro, conquistador of Peru, this remote community his home town.

Thornton Wilder at the Century

At *Time: The Weekly Newsmagazine*, my editor's name was Alfred Thornton Baker, and he was related in some way to the playwright and novelist Thornton Wilder. Spontaneously, one morning at the office, Baker appeared at the edge of my cubicle, and said, "You need a little glamour in your life—come have lunch with Thornton Wilder." We walked seven blocks south and one over to the

Century Association, where Wilder had arrived before us. Baker may have been counting on me to be some sort of buffer. I was about thirty but I felt thirteen, and I was moon-, star-, and awestruck in the presence of the author of *Our Town*, *The Skin of Our Teeth*, and *The Bridge of San Luis Rey*. I had read and seen those and more, and had watched my older brother as Doc Gibbs in a Princeton High School production of *Our Town*. I knew stories of Wilder as a young teacher at the Lawrenceville School, five miles from Princeton, pacing in the dead of night on the third floor of Davis House above students quartered below.

"What is that?"

"Mr. Wilder. He's writing something."

About halfway through the Century lunch, Baker asked Wilder the question writers hear four million times in a lifespan if they die young: "What are you working on?"

Wilder said he was not actually writing a new play or novel but was fully engaged in a related project. He was cataloguing the plays of Lope de Vega.

Lope de Vega wrote some eighteen hundred full-length plays. Four hundred and thirty-one survive. How long would it take to read four hundred and thirty-one plays? How long would it take to summarize each in descriptive detail and fulfill the additional requirements of cataloguing? So far having said nothing, I was thinking these things. How long would it take the Jet Propulsion Lab to get something crawling on a moon of Neptune? Wilder was sixty-six, but to me he appeared and sounded geriatric. He was an old man with a cataloguing project that would take him at least a dozen years. Callowly, I asked him, "Why would anyone want to do that?"

Wilder's eyes seemed to condense. Burn. His face turned fu-
rious. He said, "Young man, do not ever question the purpose of
scholarship."

I went catatonic for the duration. To the end, Wilder remained
cold. My blunder was as naïve as it was irreparable. Nonetheless,
at that time in my life I thought the question deserved an answer.
And I couldn't imagine what it might be.

I can now. I am eighty-eight years old at this writing and I
know that those four hundred and thirty-one plays were serving
to extend Thornton Wilder's life. Reading them and cataloguing
them was something to do, and do, and do. It beat dying. It was
a project meant not to end.

I could use one of my own. And why not? With the same ul-
terior motive, I could undertake to describe in capsule form the
many writing projects that I have conceived and seriously planned
across the years but have never written.

By the way, did you ever write about Extremadura?

No, but I'm thinking about it.

At current velocities, it takes twelve years to get to the moons
of Neptune. On that day at the Century Association, Thornton
Wilder had twelve years to live.

The Moons of Methuselah

George H. W. Bush jumped out of airplanes on octo birthdays.
Some people develop their own Presidential libraries without
experiencing a prior need to be President. For offspring and ex-

tended families, old people write books about their horses, their houses, their dogs, and their cats, published at the kitchen table. Old-people projects keep old people old. You're no longer old when you're dead.

Mark Twain's old-person project was his autobiography, which he dictated with regularity when he was in his seventies. He had a motive that puts it in a category by itself. For the benefit of his daughters, he meant to publish it in parts, as appendices to his existing books, in order to extend the copyrights beyond their original expiration dates and his. The bits about Hannibal and his grammar-school teacher Mrs. Horr, for example, could be tacked onto *The Adventures of Tom Sawyer*, while untold items from his river-pilot years could be appended to *Life on the Mississippi*. Repeatedly he tells his reader how a project such as this one should be done—randomly, without structure, in total disregard of consistent theme or chronology. Just jump in anywhere, tell whatever comes to mind from any era. If something distracts your memory and seems more interesting at the moment, interrupt the first story and launch into the new one. The interrupted tale can be finished later. That is what he did, and the result is about as delicious a piece of writing as you are ever going to come upon, and come upon, and keep on coming upon, as it draws you in for the rest of your life. If ever there was an old-man project, this one was the greatest. It is only seven hundred and thirty-five thousand words long. If Mark Twain had stayed with it, he would be alive today.

When I was in my prime, I planned to write about a dairy farm in Indiana with twenty-five thousand cows. Now, taking my cue from George Bush, Thornton Wilder, and countless others who stayed hale doing old-person projects, I am writing about not writing about the dairy farm with twenty-five thousand cows. Not to mention Open Doctors, golf-course architects who alter existing courses to make them fit for upcoming U.S. Opens and the present game—lengthening holes, moving greens, rethinking bunkers. Robert Trent Jones was the first Open Doctor, and his son Rees is the most prominent incumbent. Fine idea for a piece, but for me, over time, a hole in zero. So I decided to describe many such saved-up, bypassed, intended pieces of writing as an old-man project of my own.

After six or seven months, however, I felt a creeping dilemma, and I confided it one day on a bike ride with Joel Achenbach, author of books on science and history, a reporter for *The Washington Post*, and a student from my writing class in 1982. Doing such a project as this one, I whined, begets a desire to publish what you write, and publication defeats the ongoing project, the purpose of which is to keep the old writer alive by never coming to an end.

Joel said, "Just call it 'Volume One.'"

"Hitler Youth"

Many decades ago, I played on a summer softball team sponsored by the Gallup Poll. Our diamond was on the campus of Princeton University, and one of my teammates was Josh Miner. Years passed, the softball with them, and I did not see Josh again until 1966, when he invited me to go with him to Hurricane Island, in Penobscot Bay.

Josh had been a math and physics teacher, a coach, and an

administrator at the Hun School, in Princeton, and by 1966 had been doing much the same at Phillips Academy, in Andover, Massachusetts. Meanwhile, though, he had gone to Scotland to teach for a time at Gordonstoun, on the Moray Firth, near Inverness. The founder and original headmaster there was Kurt Hahn, who had been the headmaster of Salem, a school in Germany, where he developed an outdoor program teaching self-reliance and survival in extreme predicaments. Fleeing the Nazis in the nineteen-thirties, he brought the program to Gordonstoun, and during the Second World War he set up a version of it in Wales that taught ocean survival skills to merchant seamen, who were being lost in great numbers from torpedoed ships. Lives were saved. Hahn called his program Outward Bound and continued to teach it at the school.

Josh came back from Scotland with it and became Outward Bound's founding director in the United States. After Colorado and Minnesota, Maine's Hurricane Island was the site of the third Outward Bound school established in this country. In 1966, it was two years old. I was in my second year as a staff writer at *The New Yorker*. Josh hoped that our stay on Hurricane Island would motivate me to write either a profile of Kurt Hahn, with Outward Bound a significant component, or vice versa.

On the way home, I stopped in New York to present these possibilities to William Shawn, to whom I have alluded as *The New Yorker*'s supreme eyeshade. I described the Outward Bound curriculum and told him about the solo, when students go off completely alone for a couple of days and nights and eat only things they are able to forage. On Hurricane Island when we were there, Euell Gibbons—a lifelong forager of wild food, the author of a best-seller called *Stalking the Wild Asparagus*—was teaching students what to look for on their solos (less of a problem in Penobscot Bay than, say, in the Estancia Valley of New Mexico, where Gibbons's boyhood foraging in years of extreme drought had kept his family alive). It had been my good luck that Shawn was particularly dedicated to long pieces of factual writing, but my luck for now ran out. Shawn was having nothing of Outward Bound. He compared it to the Hitler Youth. He said Euell Gibbons sounded interesting, and suggested that I do a profile of Gibbons instead. Which I did, going down the Susquehanna River and a section of the Appalachian Trail—eating what we foraged—in November of that year.

The Bridges of Christian Menn

Sinuous, up in the sky between one mountainside and another, the most beautiful bridge I had ever seen was in Simplon Pass, on the Swiss side. It fairly swam through the air, now bending right, now left, its deck held up by piers and towers, one of which was very nearly five hundred feet high. A bridge I saw in Bern, also in stressed concrete, was strikingly beautiful and reminded me of the one at Simplon. I was in Switzerland through the autumn of 1982, having arranged to accompany in their annual service the Section de Renseignements of Battalion 8, Regiment 5, Mountain Division 10, Swiss Army. When I returned to Princeton toward the end of November, I couldn't wait to see my friend David Billington, a professor of civil engineering, who was absorbed by the art in engineering and the engineering in art.

Breathlessly, and pretty damned naïvely—thinking I was telling him something he might not know—I said I had seen a bridge at Simplon Pass that was a spectacular work of art and another in Bern that reminded me of it. Puzzlingly, because he wasn't speaking in print, he said, "They are bridges of Christian Menn." Christian Menn, he explained, was a Swiss structural engineer unparalleled in the world as a designer of bridges. Moreover, Billington continued, he had a remarkable coincidence to reveal, given where I had been and what I had seen. While I was with the Swiss Army and admiring the structures of Christian Menn, he, Billington, had presented at the Princeton University Art Museum an exhibit of scale models of the bridges of Christian Menn. He'd be happy to show me the models.

Shortly afterward, Billington published a book called *The Tower and the Bridge: The New Art of Structural Engineering*, with a picture of the Simplon bridge on the dust jacket. He brought Menn to Princeton to lecture on—what else?—bridges. Menn was a professor of structural engineering at the Swiss Federal Institute of Technology, in Zurich, where Albert Einstein got his diploma in math and natural sciences, where the mathematician John von Neumann got his in chemical engineering, and where the China-born paleoclimatologist Ken Hsü got his umlaut.

Menn's Felsenau Viaduct, in Bern, was eight years old when I first saw it, his bridge at Simplon only two. In years that followed, I would come upon the Bunker Hill Memorial Bridge, over the Charles River, in Boston, pure magic with its optical pyramids of cables coming down from its towers directly to the deck (a so-called cable-stayed bridge), and the soaring Sunniberg Bridge, in the canton of Graubunden, and more bridges designed by

Christian Menn. He finished his lecture at Princeton with blue-prints and conceptual drawings of the bridge of a lifetime, an old-man project outdoing the plays of Lope de Vega or jumping out of airplanes. This was a cable-stayed suspension bridge crossing the Strait of Messina, between Sicily and the Italian mainland. At two miles, its central span would be the longest in the world, three-quarters of a mile longer than the incumbent, the Akashi-Kaikyo Bridge, in Japan, which connects Kobe with an island in Osaka Bay. Back in the day, the Roman Republic developed plans for a bridge across the Strait of Messina. The Repubblica Italiana may get around to it in two or three thousand years.

Having conceived of the largest bridge in the world, Menn went on to compete for one of the smallest. Princeton University was completing a group of four science buildings, two on either side of Washington Road, which belongs to Mercer County and bisects the Princeton campus in a dangerous way. The danger is to drivers who might run over students, who, staring into their phones, characteristically ignore the heavy traffic, not to mention the traffic lights, and seem to look upon Washington Road as an outdoor pedestrian mall. The four buildings house the labs and classrooms of Physics and Chemistry, on the east side of the road, and Genomics and Neuroscience, on the west. A footbridge would, among other things, save lives. This was not a rialto over Monet's lily pads. Crossing the fast vehicular traffic, it had four destinations. Professor Billington offered the university an im-modest suggestion. Since the footbridge design was in such need of an elegant solution, why not engage one of the greatest bridge designers in the history of the world? The university said that if Billington's Swiss friend was interested in the job he would have to enter a competition like everybody else. Menn was interested in the job and he took part in the competition. Oddly, he won. His footbridge is shaped like a pair of parentheses back to back:)(. The two sides flow together at an apex over the road, and its four extremities diverge, respectively, to Neuroscience, Genomics, Physics, and Chemistry.

For every time I cross that bridge on foot, I cross it about a hundred times on my bicycle. More often than not, as I go up and down its curves, I am reminded not only that this wee bridge— along with the Ganter Bridge at Simplon and the Felsenau, in Bern, and the Sunniberg, in Graubunden, and the Bunker Hill Memorial, in Boston—is one of the bridges of Christian Menn, but also that I have never written a lick about him, or about David Billington, or a profile of Billington containing a long set piece on Menn, or a profile of Menn containing a long set piece on Billington, or a fifty-fifty profile of them together, which I intended from my Swiss days in the Section de Renseignements through the decades that have followed. David Billington died in 2018, as did Christian Menn.

The Airplane That Crashed in the Woods

After dark on a May evening in 1985, I was driving home from work and was about half a mile up the small road I live on when my way was blocked by a pile of tree limbs, wires among them, ripped from utility poles. Drizzly rain was falling through light fog. I stopped, stepped out, and tried to see if there was a way to get past without being electrocuted. I heard a sound in the woods like the wailing of an animal, which is what I thought it was, although I had heard all kinds of animals wailing in those woods and this was not like them. There was no way to proceed. I turned the car around, went back a short distance to a neighbor's house, and called the township police.

I returned to the wires and the tree limbs, and had scarcely stopped, or so it seemed, when a police car followed me, and two officers got out, heard the wailing sound, and went into the woods. They were Jack Petrone, the Chief of Police, and his son Jackie. Jack had been a basketball player in high school. So had I—same high school, three years apart. He came out of the woods before long, leading and supporting a woman with a severely damaged leg. A calf muscle had been stripped from the bone and hung down in a large flap like a cow's tongue. Jack tossed to me a roll of adhesive bandage, said, "Put that back in place," and returned quickly to the woods.

In my youth, I was particularly squeamish about blood. When I was in college, I fainted while donating it. Now I had been told to put a detached calf muscle back where it came from, which I did, as gently as I could. The woman it belonged to bravely kept the pain to herself. Her home was in Hopewell Township, several miles west, and I did not know her, or her husband, or the couple they were travelling with, one of whom was the pilot of the Cessna they had crashed in. He was the worst hurt, mainly trauma to the head, and he was the reason for Jack Petrone's hurried return to the woods. It seemed incredible, but everyone survived.

The two men and two women had been playing golf in Myrtle Beach. Their Cessna was based at Princeton Airport, a small field for light planes, three beeline miles northeast of the crash site. The pilot was flying under Instrument Flight Rules, with foul weather all the way from South Carolina to New Jersey. The I.F.R. route from Myrtle Beach to Princeton proceeded northeast from way-point to waypoint and not at all on a beeline. After the waypoint nearest Trenton, the I.F.R. route went north before doubling back for Princeton, adding about fifty miles to the journey. Princeton is ten miles from Trenton. The pilot gained permission to bank right, abandon his I.F.R. flight plan, and go for Princeton under Visual Flight Rules. V.F.R. required, among other things, that he not fly in cloud, and that his minimum horizontal visibility be about three miles. The elevation of Trenton is forty-nine feet. The elevation of Princeton Airport is a hundred and twenty-five feet. The wooded ridge I live on is four hundred feet high.

The weather cleared, and for a week after the crash the air above our road was filled with light aircraft—not actually a swarm, like mosquitoes looking for blood, but quite a few of them, rubber-necking, perhaps apprehensively, curious to discern whatever they thought they could discern. A few days later, in a Princeton restau-rant, a couple my wife and I knew named Daphne and Dudley Hawkes stopped by our table as they were leaving. Dudley, an orthopedic surgeon and a pilot of light aircraft, wanted to know everything we could tell him about the accident on our road. All I could tell him would become what I have written here.

Four months later, Dudley took off from Robbinsville Airport, near Trenton, in a rented Mooney 201 on his way by himself to Parents' Day at Hamilton College. He plowed into an embank-ment beside Route 130, and died.

Daphne was an Episcopal priest, the first of her gender in New Jersey. In 1984, she had spent three hours with my writing stu-dents at Princeton University, whose assignment for that week was to interview her as a group and then individually write profiles of her. The result would be sixteen varying portraits built from one set of facts. Daphne parked her car close by, on Nassau Street, and after she left the classroom and returned to the car she got into an argument with a woman in the next parking space, who thought her vehicle, in some fender-bending or related way, had been threatened by Daphne's. The heat rose, crescendoed, strong words flying, until the offended woman shouted, "Would I not tell the truth? Would I lie to you? I am a rabbi."

Daphne was wearing a wool vest that closed high, in the manner of a turtleneck. She reached up with one finger and pulled it down, exposing her clerical collar.

A few years later—at an event in Trenton honoring Senator Bill Bradley—the two women were brought together again, one to give the invocation, the other the closing prayer. Someone asked them, "Have you met?"

Daphne said, "We've run into each other."

The people from Hopewell Township who crashed on our road sued Cessna for—as I understood the complaint—not making a cockpit of sufficient structure to withstand the forces that injured them. I was subpoenaed to testify. There would be a deposition in my office in East Pyne Hall, on the Princeton campus. My office was not a boardroom. It sorely lacked space for me, two lawyers, and a court stenographer. We were crowded in there for upwards of an hour, and I learned early on that I was meant to testify but not to tell a story. I was bubbling mad. How could anyone even imagine suing Cessna for Cessna's role in the crash? As the court stenographer tapped along, I tried to say as much, but was quieted by the lawyers as my words were inserted edgewise.

This seemed to be a story to tell, to investigate, to amplify, to enrich with detail about flight rules, liability law, aircraft design, women priests, women rabbis, and varying portraits of one subject by sixteen writers, but beyond this brief outline the disparate parts of "The Airplane That Crashed in the Woods" seemed as resistant to the weaving and telling as they had been with an audience of two lawyers and a court stenographer.

On the Campus

When I was nine, ten years old, I knew where every urinal was on the Princeton campus. They are among my earliest memories. There were so many of them that they also represent the greatest sources of instant gratification that I have ever known. We (there were others like me) also knew where the pool tables were, and went from place to place until we found one free of students. Most of all, I dribbled my outdoor basketball across the campus and down the slate walks to the gym, where we went in the front door if it was open and in a basement window if not. The campus gradually absorbs a campus rat. When I was ten, and after the Japanese attacked Pearl Harbor, I soon got into an air-spotter course taught in a lecture hall in the Frick Chemistry Lab. My grade school, which has since become a university building, was close by and on the same street. The main purpose of the course was to train people to identify Nazi warplanes seen above New Jersey, and to report them by telephone to the regional headquarters of the U.S. Army Ground Observer Corps. The trainees were, for the most part, middle-aged women and little boys. We, the latter, were not in much need of the training, being completely familiar, from magazines and books, with the styles and silhouettes of the world's military airplanes. But the course was fun, like some precursive television show, as the black silhouette of an aircraft came up on a large screen and was gone two seconds later while you were writing down its name. Messerschmitt ME-109. Next slide, two seconds: Mitsubishi Zero. Next slide, two seconds: Grumman Avenger. Next slide, two seconds: Vought-Sikorsky Corsair. Yes, the American planes were the only planes we would ever report to regional headquarters, in New York or somewhere, in a cryptic sequence from a filled-in, columned sheet: "one, bi, low," and so forth—one twin-engined plane flying low, often a DC-3 descending to Newark. We saw Piper Cubs, Stinson Reliants, and more DC-3s. We saw Martin Marauders, Curtiss-Wright Warhawks, Republic Thunderbolts, Bell Airacobras, Lockheed Lightnings, Consolidated Liberators. It would be treason to say that we were eager to see Heinkel HE-111s and Dornier DO-17s. We didn't really know what was going on. We were ten, eleven years old and not regarded as precocious.

I can't see fish in a river but I could see airplanes in the sky, and what I wouldn't have given for an ME-109, as long as it was destroyed after we made the phone call. In case the British attacked, we were prepared to identify them, too. Next slide, two seconds: Supermarine Seafire. Next slide, two seconds: Supermarine Spitfire. What a name—the aircraft that won the Battle of Britain. Bristol Beaufort, Bristol Beaufighter, Hawker Hurricane, Hawker Typhoon, de Havilland Mosquito, Gloster Gladiator, Vickers Wellington. But we were there because we knew from Fokker, and Fokker from Focke-Wulf. Ilyushin, Tupolev, Lavochkin, Mikoyan-Gurevich. Next . . .

The middle-aged women were people with cars, who could

drive the little boys to country sheds and shacks set up by the
Aircraft Warning Service, a civilian component of the Army's
Ground Observer Corps. I don't mean to downsize the women
or their role in all this, but—Mrs. Hall, Mrs. Hambling—they
didn't know a Focke-Wulf 200 from a white-throated sparrow.
They were totally frank about it and relied on us to name the
planes. Mrs. Hambling, who was English, picked me up at school.
I rode my bike to Mrs. Hall's house, a beautiful place on Snowden
Lane. They both took me to a very small hut on the edge of a farm
near Rocky Hill, and drove me back to Princeton hours later. I
still have my AWS arm band—red, white, blue, and gold, with
wings.

When I was in high school, I worked for the university's Department of Biology, in Guyot Hall. It was a great job, not only
for its variety but because I could make my own hours, riding
there on my bicycle to do pre-set chores. This allowed me to
hold a job and also to be on Princeton High School's basketball and tennis teams. For Professor Chase—Aurin M. Chase, a
biochemist—I copied scientific papers. This was years before Xerox.
There were no photocopiers. The papers were copied by a photo-
stat machine, which took pictures of them on photographic paper,
which, in a photographic darkroom, was immersed, one page at
a time, in a fluid called developer. You gazed down into the fluid
and watched as words and images chemically appeared. Professor
Chase taught me how to do that. It was slow going. Even to copy
a relatively short paper, "Proc Nat Ac Sci"—"Proceedings of the
National Academy of Sciences"—could take the better part of an
hour. For Professor Arthur Parpart, whose principal interest was
in the physiological and biochemical architecture of red-blood-
cell membranes, I cleaned the beef blood out of his centrifuge. I

stuffed wads of cotton into my nostrils. After beef blood has been centrifugally subdivided and left in metal test tubes awhile, its smell could level a city. During the recent world war, a research project he directed helped to increase the maximum storage time of human blood from three days to thirty. From Professor Gerhard Fankhauser, I learned to smell the difference between alcohol and formaldehyde, a useful talent in Princeton. In Professor Fankhauser's lab were many large jars—glass, heavy, maybe fourteen inches high and about that in diameter—containing marine specimens. Starfish. Octopuses. Vicious-looking eels. Each jar had a glass lid like a manhole cover, sealed with beeswax. Some specimens were in alcohol, others in formaldehyde. Gradually, despite the beeswax, the fluids in the jars had gone down and needed to be topped up. My job was to open a jar, sniff the contents, replace the alcohol or formaldehyde, seal the jar with new beeswax, and move on to the next jar.

When I was fourteen, a recurrent vision would enter my mind as I drowned fruit flies in the Guyot basement. This is what happens when you die: In the immediate afterlife, you are confronted by every macroscopic creature you killed in your earthbound lifetime. They have an afterlife, too. They come at you as a massive crowd, which, in my case, would consist of ants, mosquitoes, yellowjackets, houseflies, fruit flies, horseflies, spiders, centipedes, cockroaches, moles, mice, shrews, snakes, trout, catfish, sand sharks, walleyes, wasps, rabbits, ticks, lampreys, leeches, ladybugs, beetles, centrarchids, annelids, American shad, Atlantic salmon, honeybees, hornets, Arctic char, Pacific salmon, pike, pickerel, caterpillars, butterflies, bluefish, moths, mullet, perch, suckers, fallfish, and bats, not to mention road-killed squirrels, raccoons, pheasants, and deer. They envelop you like a cloud, a fog that bites.

To be sure, I was still in the up phase of growing up, but while the fruit flies went on dying, the spiritual concept did not. Did Goliath have a second chance at David? Did Hamilton have another shot at Burr? Did the unknown German meet the Unknown Soldier? I wouldn't want to be some people I knew in bush Alaska. When they, lying in bed at night, saw a leg or a proboscis coming through the webbing of a net around them, they pinched the leg or the proboscis and pulled it out of the mosquito on the other side. I wouldn't want to be Ian Frazier. He wolfs down living mayflies. The University of Pennsylvania once gave him a box of chocolate-covered insects, which some regarded as an honorary degree. In his benign and gentle manner, he is broadly looked upon as a type who would not hurt a flea, but I would not want to be that flea.

I killed the fruit flies for Kenneth Cooper, whose lab was up on the second floor, where he and his wife, Ruth, geneticists, raised them in half-pint glass milk bottles. Each bottle had a few centimeters of gelatinous cereal at the bottom and was stoppered with a wad of cotton. In this environment, a generation of *Drosophila melanogaster* would develop quickly. The Coopers anesthetized them, shook them out under amplifying glass, and recorded the varying colors of their eyes. They scraped up the sleeping generation and returned it to its birthplace. The fruit flies woke up and jumped around. I took them downstairs to a janitorial closet in trays, a hundred and forty-four bottles in a tray—conservatively, three thousand fruit flies per tray. There was a big sink, deeper than wide, in the closet. One bottle at a time, I removed the cotton wad and held the bottle under a stream of falling water. I poured the dead flies into the sink to ride off into the Princeton sewer system, then removed the gelatinous cereal with a long, iron fork. I was not expert at any aspect of this procedure. The janitors hated me. In each generation of flies, an estimated twenty per cent got away while I was handling them. I nonetheless murdered most of them, and I am not ready to face them.

As it happens, my office today, seventy-five years later, is in Guyot Hall—actually, on the roof of Guyot Hall, in what I have elsewhere described as a fake medieval turret. Guyot is and was shared fifty-fifty by Geology and Biology. My turret belongs to Geosciences—the department that took me in as an enduring guest when the building I previously worked in was evacuated for complete refurbishment. My father's principal office on the campus was in the building next door. Looking down from my arrow-slit windows, I can see it.

The Guilt of the U.S. Male

My high-school class was graduated in the McCarter Theater, on the Princeton campus—pomp, circumstance, the whole eight yards. Prizes were given. There was one—a hundred-dollar check from a sponsoring bank—for the academically top-ranked boy. Under my mortarboard, under my tassel, suddenly rich, I was the top-ranked boy. I was sixth in the class. Estelle Groom, the top girl, got a hundred dollars, too. Ann Durell, Nancy Cawley, Patricia McCabe, and one other, whose name I don't remember, got nothing. Of the five, I remember where all but the one went to college. Wellesley, Mount Holyoke, Albertus Magnus . . . At some point, years later, I could have tracked them down, described their careers and families, and apologized. It didn't cross my mind until I had met Thornton Wilder.

Extremadura

Jane was exactly halfway in age between my father and me. She was my father's first cousin, and my first cousin once removed. In Ohio, she grew up Jane Roemer. As a Hollywood actress, she was Jane Randolph. After marrying a rich Spanish man, she was Jane del Amo. They lived in Madrid, and also had a house on the Castilian coast west of Santander. I met her when I was twenty-three and was spending a grad year at the University of Cambridge. There were three eight-week terms in the Cambridge year. This astonished me—a university on vacation more than half the year. I spent those long vacs in Austria, Portugal, and, for the most part, Spain.

I met Jane for the first time early one April morning, after I had spent an almost wholly sleepless night sitting in a train compartment. She picked me up at a Madrid station, and said we were going to lunch near Toledo, and we drove south. Full of energy, she was also full of talk, and no shy cousin would ever be too much for her. In Toledo, she stopped long enough to take me through the Casa del Greco and comment on the effects that astigmatism can have on works of art. Then on we went to a ranch by the river Tagus where friends of hers raised fighting bulls. In a couple of Land Rovers, we rode with four or five others among the fighting bulls. Before they meet their fate, they must never see a dismounted human being, but it was all right to get next to them in Land Rovers. One of our number was a poet whose name I think I remember as Rocio Marega, but I can't find her on the Internet or anywhere else, and Jane is no longer here to tell me. Sufficiently distant from the nearest fighting bull, we stopped by the river, got out, and sat down on the right bank to listen as the poet recited her poetry. Behind us not far was the view of Toledo, a low hump and a comparatively unaspiring tessellation of rooftops, seen from where El Greco did not see it that way. The poet was extremely good-looking, and her words came over us in a Spanish so slow, rhythmic, and lush that I almost understood them and almost fell into the river. We adjourned for lunch, indoors, in a U-shaped villa, at a long table that could have seated twenty. Afterward, the men got up, went into a hallway, and came back with shotguns. They went into the courtyard framed by the U and pointed the guns toward the sky, and one of them fired into the air. A cloud of pigeons came up from the roofs on either side. Bang. Pow. Bang. Pow. Pigeons rained down at our feet.

I spent that summer in Spain, with other American students, driving around in a surplus Jeep from the Second World War that I had bought in London. Moving slowly from Spanish town to Spanish town in the absence of bypassing four-lane highways was an experience that is now as defunct as the Underwood 5. No cell phones, no G.P.S., no computers. Town after town, you went in through the outskirts among increasingly compacting streets and into the Centro, the Plaza Mayor, then out in the same manner. There was no alternative. Kids ran along beside the Jeep shouting "El hay, el hay, el hay!" El Jeep. In regions and kingdoms of

Iberia, today leadenly called "autonomous communities," we went to Aragon, Navarra, Vizcaya, León, Castilla la Nueva, Castilla la Vieja, Valencia, Murcia, and Andalucía, but not to Extremadura. My friends preferred playing basketball in Granada to watching cork oaks breaking no sweat.

Extremadura is larger than Maryland and somewhat smaller than Vermont and New Hampshire combined. It is the exact size of Switzerland. After the 1967 trip with my family, when we traversed Extremadura south to north on our way to visit Jane and Jaime at Suances, near Santander, I kept thinking about Extremadura as a subject for a piece in *The New Yorker*, the sort of thing I had done about the Pine Barrens of New Jersey, and would do about Alaska and Wyoming. I kept thinking of the storks in the church towers of almost every Extremaduran town. I kept thinking of the cork of those oaks—six inches thick. I kept thinking of the dehesa, the vast dry woodlands with fighting bulls in them and jamón ibérico hogs, and trees spread out like checkers on a board. I proposed the idea to William Shawn, and he said, "Oh. Oh, yes." But I went to Alaska. I went to Wyoming. And although I had been obsessed with the subject since 1954, I never took my notebooks to Extremadura.

I did make a trip there in 2010. My daughter Jenny was living in London and invited us to join her family on a short vacation in—of all places—Trujillo in Extremadura. Jenny's husband is Italian, and they would be visiting another international couple (American-Spanish), who were friends in London and had a house in a rural setting on Trujillo's outskirts. Yolanda, my wife, was booked to visit other daughters in the opposite direction, so I went to Spain alone. We were three generations there, from three countries. The fossil layer included specimens from New Jersey, Vermont, and Madrid. The American-Spanish couple were Jake Donavan and Gracia Lafuente, whose father, Jaime Lafuente, was the restoration architect of the Museo del Prado. He was warm and fascinating, as was the whole scene. In small units—Jenny and I, Jenny and I and her fourteen-year-old son, Tommaso, Jenny and I and Gracia—we made day trips on multiple vectors to towns and small cities of Extremadura. In Trujillo, we went to a compact, elegant restored house that had been the boyhood home of Francisco de Orellana, born in Trujillo in 1511. Pizarro, still on his horse in the Plaza Mayor, might have moved over. In December, 1541, on a mountain stream in the Andes, de Orellana and a crew got into a small boat and travelled east, downstream, intent to see where the current would take them. After eight months, it had taken them to the Atlantic Ocean. En route, they had built a larger boat—a brigantine—appropriate for the ever-widening waters, and they were attacked by a tribal force that included women warriors. There was education aplenty aboard the brigantine. In Greek mythology, warrior women were known as Amazons. That was the first known journey from mountains to mouth through the Amazon watershed.

In a plaza in Jerez de los Caballeros, a village in southwestern Extremadura, is a statue of Vasco Núñez de Balboa. His home town. He, too, could move over. Jerez de los Caballeros was also the home town of Hernando de Soto, about twenty years younger and also born in the late fifteenth century. When Balboa "discovered" the Pacific Ocean, in 1513, he claimed all of it for Spain. De Soto began his exploration of North America in 1539. Always looking for gold, he travelled extensively in what is now the southeastern United States, and eventually crossed the Mississippi River—the first European to do so. He succumbed to fever on the western bank. De Soto and Balboa both died in their middle forties.

A little younger than Balboa and a little older than de Soto was Hernán Cortés, who made vassals of the Aztecs. Cortés was born and reared in Medellín, province of Badajoz, in Extremadura. Wikipedia, in reference to this sixteenth-century bloom of conquistadores, says of Extremadura that its "difficult conditions pushed many of its ambitious young men to seek their fortunes overseas." You can wik that again. Who would not think twice about living out life on this remote, landlocked, desiccated ground?

Well . . . Roman soldiers. Mérida, the capital of Extremadura, was the capital of Roman Lusitania two thousand years ago. The city was founded as a retirement and long-term-care center for the 5th and 10th Legions. The name of Mérida derives from the Latin *emeritus*. Not that the Romans all just sat around. Tommaso, Jenny, and I had lunch in the peristyle of an extant Roman villa in Mérida, and afterward walked on the longest Roman bridge remaining in the world, its arches crossing the Guadiana River. Two Roman dams in tributary streams still hold back the two Roman reservoirs. A Roman aqueduct stands high but dry. Amphitheater. Circus Maximus. Triumphal arch. Temple of Diana— its length divided by eight evenly spaced Corinthian columns, its width by six. You walk among all this, look up, and expect to see the legionnaires.

Deriving from the Arabic *wadi*, for "valley," the "Guad" in Spanish geographical names denotes a river—Guadiana, Guadalupe,

Guadalete, Guadalquivir (Wadi al-Kabir). The Guadiana flows west across Extremadura through Mérida and Badajoz before bending south and eventually forming part of the boundary between Spain and Portugal all the way to the Atlantic. The Sierra de Guadalcanal straddles the Extremadura-Andalucía border, and the village and valley of Guadalcanal are on the Andalusian side. The name went to the Solomon Islands in 1568, and, in 1942, into the vocabulary of everyone on earth who was even faintly aware of the events of the war in the South Pacific. Alburquerque, northwest of Mérida and close to Portugal, lost an "r" on its way to New Mexico. In the sixteenth century, Chile was known as Nueva Extremadura. The place-name itself—Extremadura—is pretty much the same in Latin and Spanish: the outermost hard place.

According to Juan Perucho and Nestor Lújan's *El libro de la cocina española*, "the cuisine of Extremadura is serious, deep and austere, as suits the country." On the final day of that 2010 visit, we went into central Trujillo seeking some of this austerity: partridge braised with truffles, leg of goat pacense, chitterling stew, gazpacho richer in contents than its Andalusian counterpart. We sat at outdoor tables, Pizarro looking on. And when the last partridge was et, the last bit of Badajoz goat, I handed the waiter a Visa card. He disappeared and after fifteen minutes had not returned. Thirty minutes. He was away almost an hour, and, when he returned, he handed me the card and said that Visa had rejected the charge. I produced a different card, and later called the bank whose number was on the first card. A sudden efflorescence of attempted charges against my card had attracted their attention, including a large attempted purchase in South America. While

Francisco Pizarro, plunderer of Peru, larger-than-life, looked on from his commensurate horse, I was being plundered in his home town.

Zoom Laude

I could have written a whole lot about students I taught, and what they became where, but I have always put down the notion, because I was never going to risk disappointing anyone, unmentioned or mentioned. In 2020 came an unforeseeable exception. Covid-19, the "new coronavirus," named for the previous year, swept the world and closed university campuses. My writing class at Princeton had great students in it, and they were all sent home on the eleventh of March.

> *A student says to me, says she,*
> *Corona crowns the faculty.*
> *Crowns, the verb, means blocks knocked off*
> *The likes of Isaac Asimov.*
> *We've been sent home to keep the tenure track*
> *Rusting on to hell and back,*
> *To spare a lot of cerebral geezers*
> *A one-way trip to municipal freezers.*
> *The students, at nineteen—*
> *As in Covid, dean!—*
> *Are something close to immune,*
> *While the professorial cootmanship is hearing a different tune.*

The eleventh of March was a Wednesday, mid-semester, and the students had just learned that they were going home. In my class, Wednesday is a day of scheduled individual conferences about their pieces of writing. We sit side by side looking down at printouts, which are covered with notes, marginalia, transpositions, nouveau commas, purged commas, structural revolutions, and low-hanging redundancies that I, pretending to be an editor, am offering in the spirit of suggestion. On that last live Wednesday, I handed the students photocopies of my pencilled scribblings, and we practiced academic distancing.

In the second half of the semester, we did our seminars on Zoom, and the students became sixteen pictures in varied levels of light. Claudia Frykberg had gone home to Woollahra, New South Wales. She got up at 4 A.M. for the seminars. Edward Tian was in Etobicoke, Ontario, Lola Wheeler in Gravesend, Kent. The thirteen others were scattered around the United States, including Julia Campbell, of Whitefish Bay, Wisconsin—she the coxswain of the Princeton men's heavyweight crew. Season cancelled.

For me, the Zooming and everything that went with it took about twice as much time as the teaching normally does. Locked down with nothing else to do, I could barely get it done. With Claudia and Lola, I did the Wednesday conferences on Zoom, but on the telephone with the rest. To enable the virtual experience, I first took my scribbled-upon copies of their papers to Princeton Printer and had them scanned and turned into pdf's. (Please don't write and tell me about the apps I could be editing with; I have yet to meet an app in an eyeshade.) Princeton Printer, 150 Nassau Street, was open for business while the university opposite was darker and emptier than the inside of a football. A sign on the sidewalk outside Princeton Printer—there as in every spring—was urging students to have their theses bound at Princeton Printer. All seniors were finishing theses, but this time at home.

My sixteen sophomores were at home writing, too. In their earlier pieces, they had pretty much been told what to write about and how, but there are no fixed requirements in the second half of the semester. Free Choice 1, Free Choice 2, they can do anything they are drawn to do as long as it is factual writing. This has produced some memorable pieces across the years. A student once wrote about bagpipers on the Staten Island Ferry, another about a Native American pow-wow in Philadelphia. Her classmate Emery Real Bird went with her. In 2015, Margaret Wright went to the subway shuttle between Grand Central Terminal and Times Square and interviewed onboard buskers who were strumming and singing to their captive audience. She was just warming up. At each end of the line, she found more buskers and learned from them their life stories—an Africa-born undergraduate from Mannes School of Music who began playing his cello under Times Square in an attempt to overcome stage fright, a Haiti-born trumpet player in Grand Central of whom she wrote: "He makes me feel, as I shuffle past dirty grey columns and black rolling suitcases, as if I am in church."

In 1981, David Montgomery went to New York intending to watch children sailing sailboats in Central Park. When he arrived, rain was falling in a cold drizzle, and there were no children, no sailboats on The Pond. Dejected, he sat down on a park bench, and wondered what to do. Soon, an untailored and unbarbered man walked up to the bench and addressed him, saying, "I am the Poet O." David was not about to confuse this man with Lord

Byron, but when the Poet O said, "For fifty cents, I will write a poem for you," David produced two quarters. In the Poet O, David had begun to see Free Choice 2. After O dashed off a poem, David handed him two more quarters. O was inspired. David began to interview him, and followed him into the subway, and downtown to the Village for a description of the digs of Poet O.

And then there was David Spitz. In 1996, as a way of getting material for a Free Choice piece, Spitz applied for admission to the Ringling Bros. and Barnum & Bailey Clown College, in Sarasota, Florida, a process that required him to be auditioned when the circus was in Madison Square Garden. In a field of several dozen candidates, he was chosen and was all but offered a scholarship. I told him ever after that he passed up a great opportunity, but he opted not to transfer.

So now, in April, 2020, my student writers—rusticated, locked down, socially distanced, sheltered in place at home—had to figure how to do Free Choice 1 and Free Choice 2. One thing they had on their hands was time. They responded with as finished and polished a set of reportorial papers as I had seen in decades of teaching.

Claudia Frykberg does two things as well as few do—her writing and her swimming. Her home, in a suburb of Sydney, is close to the ocean. She has competed for Princeton in multiple events, strokes, and distances. She is a two-hundred-meter freestyler, and also races freestyle at incremental distances up to 1,650 meters—one and a hair miles. She competes in backstroke, breaststroke, individual medley. And now, in lockdown in Australia, with her Free Choice pieces due April 3 and 17, she first wrote about underwater rugby, a sport that seems to require—if this is possible—

about six times as much energy as water polo. She could do that without getting wet. Worried about the lockdown's assault on her physical conditioning, she went to the rock pools of New South Wales. Bondi Beach, for one, was a few minutes due east of her home, Bronte Beach not far, Freshwater Beach up the coast near the famous Manly. These crescent beaches are typically backed by sheer cliffs, and against the cliffs are concrete pools with seawater in them—rectangular, the ends fifty meters apart. Day after day before dawn, she went to one rock pool or another and dove in, writing her story in her head as she swam.

> Each stroke I took was effortless. I was cutting swathes through a liquid cocoon—cold, but strangely comforting. The motion was mechanical, my mind was empty. I stopped at the wall to lift my head and take a few deep breaths. I felt alone. But this wasn't the same type of alone I had grown accustomed to, symptomatic of weeks spent confined in a small space, cut off from the rest of the world in a country that I hadn't called home in close to two years. In this solitude, I found freedom and solace. A true paradox—one form of loneliness remedying another.

Zoom doesn't give a damn where somebody is. Zoom doesn't know from New South Wales, Zoom doesn't know from New Jersey. Priya Vulchi's home is in Princeton. She was born in Princeton. She is a graduate of Princeton High School. This set of facts exactly aligns with the résumé of your correspondent. We were both born on Witherspoon Street, in the old hospital. At the end of her senior year at PHS, Priya and her classmate Winona Guo deferred their admission to Princeton and Harvard, and took a gap year to travel the United States and interview teen-agers about race, politics, climate, and justice. In September, 2018, as they matriculated at the two universities, they submitted their book, *Tell Me Who You Are*. Published in 2019, it is a substantial compendium. It weighs three pounds. And now, second semester of sophomore year, Priya was sent the few blocks home. What to write, alone in Princeton? First, she went into an even deeper well and wrote emotionally about the death of her dog. Then she pulled herself together and started calling college friends shut away in their own homes all over the United States. She also called kids who appear in her book. From Atlanta, Bridgeport, Pittsburgh, Providence, New Orleans, Ann Arbor, San Mateo, Austin, and Rapid City, she assembled a montage of quotes and descriptions in answer to a single question: What is it like in lockdown with your parents?

Don't ask.

Ian McInnis, of Virginia, living in Austin, Texas, studied a book a girlfriend recommended on couples courting fully dressed in bed: *The Art of Bundling: Being an Inquiry Into the Nature & Origins of That Curious But Universal Folk-Custom, With an Exposition of the Rise & Fall of Bundling in the Eastern Part of North America*. Amazon, hardcover, $4.09. It made a lot of sense if a country boy walked a distance from his farm to spend the evening with a girl and, thanks to bundling, did not have to walk home, often in snow, late at night. Shoes off, clothes intact, further and separately wrapped in sheets, he and she spent the night in bed, sometimes in her parents' bedroom. Ian's friend with the sophisticated recommendation was sheltered in a place other than Austin, however, and all he had was the book. To find his other Free Choice piece, he unsequestered himself and went outside to see what "essential businesses" were open. In south Austin was an essential business with a sign overhead so high that it could be seen from miles away. PAWN SHOP. When Ian walked into the place—Mustang Jewelry & Pawn—he was preceded by "a guy with two daughters and an ankle monitor." Covid-19 had caused a run on the gun racks, which Michael Doss, the proprietor, thought "quite comical, 'cause you can't buy any bullets—it's like toilet paper."

Like half the journalists on the planet at this time, Kenny Peng wrote about toilet paper. Kenny Peng, of Pleasanton, California, near San Francisco Bay, is a math major. He wrote at greater length and in greater scientific detail than the professionals, not to mention his blow-by-blow accounts of toilet-paper violence in supermarkets. Moving on to his next, and less difficult, subject, he encapsulated Euclidean geometry and explained triangle centers to his lay readership, holding to the end the interest of the innumerate (e.g., me). Among thousands of different types of triangle centers, the centroid kind is the most straightforward. Lines drawn from each vertex to the midway point in a triangle's opposite side intersect in one place. No matter the shape of the triangle, or how ungainly it may be, the three lines always cross one another at a single point. As Kenny went to virtual press, the number of triangle centers so far known in the mathematical history of the world was 37,887 and growing.

Edward Tian, sheltered at home in Ontario, wrote of helping his grandmother, in her eighties, struggling three hours a day to learn English. As Edward's structure and narrative work their way backward in time, his grandmother, ever younger, becomes what she was. English is her third language, Russian her second. She grew up in Dalian, a coastal city in Liaoning Province, founded by Russians in 1898. An electrical and electronic engineer, she was trained at Tsinghua University, in Beijing. She became expert in television-broadcasting systems, and was instrumental in bringing the Chinese system forward to equality with others in the world.

> "High Five, I do not understand," she tells me. So we demonstrate, our hands meeting in mid-air. She holds onto mine, and for a moment she doesn't let go.

Ellen Li, from Millburn, New Jersey, forty miles from Princeton, speaks in a low and tentative voice that tends to veil her feistiness and her elevated perspicacity. As a patient with chronic fatigue syndrome, she came to class in an electric wheelchair in the first half of the semester. In the Zoom phase, when an upper-middle-aged visitor to our virtual seminar was searching his mind helplessly for a name he could not remember, Ellen said, "Noam Chomsky." Sheltered in Millburn, she wrote about her beloved grandfather—"an old Chinese guy who doesn't speak English" after twenty-five years in the United States—and her attempts to help him from her childhood forward. When she is six and seven years old, he takes her to soccer practices and games, and afterward to Häagen-Dazs, where he orders bo ta pi kong ice cream for both of them, hers in a kapu, his in a kong. In patient, tender dialogue, her efforts to teach him are tireless. His all-purpose word is "hey." He becomes famous in Essex County for his uncanny skill at catching fish in the Rahway River. The Old Chinese Fisherman Fan Club is established on the Internet. A post reads: "Today I asked the old Chinese fisherman, 'How many fish did you catch today?' and he said 'Hey!'" He asks Ellen how to pronounce Rahway. In his inability to do so, he is right at home in New Jersey.

Lola Wheeler, in England, wrote a piece on her polyglot family. Locked down at a desk in an upstairs hallway, she faces her brother, on the other side of the desk. Her brother studied in Malaysia, and peppers his English with the Malaysian suffix "lah." How are you today, lah? This bloody virus is beastly inconvenient, lah. He is talented at speaking English as if it is his second language. Meanwhile, after a year and three-quarters at Princeton, Lola is regarded by her family as a visitor with an American accent. Her mother has lived in Gravesend almost all her life. Lola's father is a Cockney taxi driver in London.

As Passover came and went, Claire Lessler, sheltered in Brooklyn, devised a piece of writing of no small complexity about Sephardic and Ashkenazi dialects as related to chanted recitations at the Passover seder—double letters, glottal stops, voiceless pharyngeal fricatives. At the table, her sister chants the Dayenu, her brother the Haggadah. "In the midst of a pandemic," Claire thinks, "the words of the Haggadah feel hollow and ironic. 'This is the eleventh plague,' my mom remarks, 'and Pharaoh is still holding us hostage.'"

Julia Campbell, in Whitefish Bay with no men's heavyweight crew to cox, was stirred to outrage by Wisconsin's primary election, which she covered with pen and mask, watching people risk their lives to vote—queued up closely and almost endlessly because they were prevented from voting by mail. After Princeton—law school.

Josephine de la Bruyere described a phenomenon that has spread like a virus through the Marine Corps base in Quantico, Virginia. To read her tell it, most Marines at Quantico are infected or are about to come down with what the Marines themselves have diagnosed as "Fiancée Fever." For example, one feverish Marine is "a high-school track star turned state-school frat star who decided at twenty-two—after four years of keg stands, beer bongs, and nights spent in shrubbery—that he wanted to be a real man." He has named his rifle Josephine. For her other Free Choice piece, she took her unicycle—yes, unicycle—to the Brooklyn Bridge and rode it west across the East River and then north up Manhattan's empty avenues and streets, recording bits of dialogue from people she passed. Security guard, in ball-cap mask: "You're what the city needs!" Skateboarder, with flying ponytail: "Girl, what the hell are you doing?" She was on her way to the Little Red Lighthouse under the George Washington Bridge, a total of seventeen miles. On Madison Avenue, at Fortieth Street, after five miles, she had seen thirteen moving cars in Manhattan.

The Delta Islands of the Great Valley

There's a passage in my book *Draft No. 4* that suggests a category of projects that abandoned me, not the other way around.

> Corporations prepare for journalists with bug spray. They are generally less approachable than, say, the F.B.I., and, if at all agreeable, take even more precautions. I had been rebuffed flatly by various companies and jilted by some that at first said yes. Vice-presidents said yes. CEOs heard about it and said no.

Vice-president: But Adolf, this guy is fangless. He's not Seymour Hersh. He's not Upton Sinclair.

Adolf: I don't care who he is. He's a journalist, and no matter what they write no journalist is ever going to do our company any kind of good.

This generalized scenario parodied an experience with the Union Oil Company of California, but the Kennecott Copper Corporation had been there already, when a vice-president had his gear packed for a hike in the Glacier Peak Wilderness of the North Cascades but his CEO told him to unpack and forget it. Almost entirely, I avoided corporations thereafter, despite such exceptions as an amiable experience with UPS, not to mention the complete reportorial access I had as a P.A.C. on a Lykes Brothers steamship down the west coast of South America. P.A.C. meant "Person in Addition to Crew." The Union Oil situation also involved a ship—Unocal's tanker Cornucopia—coming into the Great Central Valley of California through the sequential estuarial bays (San Francisco Bay, Grizzly Bay, San Pablo Bay, Suisun Bay) and then crossing the Sacramento–San Joaquin River Delta on its way upstream to Sacramento.

Rivers that come together to form a common delta, like the Sacramento and the San Joaquin, are extremely rare in the world—the Tigris and the Euphrates, the Ganges and the Brahmaputra, the Kennebec and the Androscoggin at Merrymeeting Bay in Maine. Rivers that come together to form a common delta in a far-inland setting are unique. In the Great Central Valley of California, the Sacramento–San Joaquin River Delta is fifty miles from the ocean.

The Central Valley is also exceptional agriculturally, providing about twenty-five per cent of American food. Until the late nineteenth century, its river deltaland was a swamp the size of Rhode Island. Big surrounding levees were built to "reclaim" land as polders—units of new farmland, below sea level, and contiguous—each consisting of thousands of acres. The polders were soon filled with fruit trees, asparagus, corn, winter wheat. Locally, they became known as islands—"the delta islands of the Great Valley."

I went there several times with Eldridge Moores, a tectonicist at the University of California (Davis), who, across fifteen years, travelled the state with me describing its geologic history. Small roads ran along the tops of the levees. From them, you looked down on the tops of pear trees in the inverted islands, looked down into the countersunk asparagus, the winter wheat. Now look up. Left, right, near, or far, you saw ships. They were crossing the delta on the rivers, which flowed between levees and were imperceptibly descending from thirteen feet above sea level (Stockton) and thirty feet above sea level (Sacramento). If you happened to be down in one of the polders among the crops, you might look up and see across a levee the wheelhouse of an oceangoing ship, inbound or outbound, sliding along against the sky. They were really up there. You had to crane your neck.

And they reminded me of a writing project I undertook in Louisiana seven years before:

> The river goes through New Orleans like an elevated highway. Jackson Square, in the French Quarter, is on high ground with respect to the rest of New Orleans, but even from the

benches of Jackson Square one looks up across the levee at the hulls of passing ships. Their keels are higher than the Astroturf in the Superdome, and if somehow the ships could turn and move at river level into the city and into the stadium, they would hover above the playing field like blimps.

Across the California delta, the ships were going southeast, upstream to Stockton, and northeast, upstream to Sacramento. We learned what was in the ships. Many thousands of bales of Kings County cotton were coming through from Stockton. Norwegian ships were taking newsprint and fertilizer to Stockton and to Sacramento. River crawdads were in ships bound for Scandinavia. Japanese ships, fitted out as sawmills, were picking up logs in Sacramento and delivering them as finished lumber in Japan. Moores's wife, Judy, told us she had read that some Japanese ships were picking up logs in Sacramento, taking them down through the delta and the bays and then to international waters two hundred miles out to sea, where they turned around and went back to Sacramento with pressed board to sell there.

I learned to pronounce Suisun "Sue Soon" and Mokelumne "McCollum Me," and—from Dale Sweetnam of California Fish and Game—that four salmon runs each year were going through the delta, essentially all chinook, the king salmon, largest of the five North American Pacific species. An occasional coho would show up, but cohos were not in the conversation. Striped bass and white sturgeon spawned in the delta and went back to the ocean. Delta smelts were uncatadromous and stayed put.

If you got off I-5 at Peltier Road, and took a service road to Woodbridge Road, you came into a wintering ground of the

sandhill crane, many hundreds around you, left and right, their
soprano gargling coming through the rain. Gray, they walked
along like ampersands, like big kiwis. They were more stately
when they stood up. Pheasants and egrets were also present, hope-
lessly outnumbered.

As with railroads, Chinese labor built the levees, and immi-
grant Chinese families formed communities on the delta islands.
One of these was Isleton, where a crawdad festival occurred each
June and orange trees were in people's yards. Another was Locke,
a redolently Chinese town, the fact notwithstanding that its principal restaurant was Al the Wop's. Al was famous for his steak
with peanut butter. In Locke there was also a deltaic museum.

The polders were built on peat, which compacted over time, and
whenever it was plowed peat dust went off with the wind. With
each new season, the polders slightly deepened—in effect, subsided.
There are a thousand miles of waterways in the delta. Many islands
were shaped to slope to center, like cisterns, and the waterways were
siphoned for irrigation. The water descended by gravity through the
fields, and was pumped back outside. Seepage through levees was
increasing the role of pumps.

But that was as nothing compared with the pumping that the
State of California was doing to keep Los Angeles—three hundred
and fifty miles and two transverse mountain ranges south—from
dying of thirst. On average, some fifteen thousand cubic feet of
water per second come down from the Sierra Nevada in Northern
California as the American, the Yuba, and the Feather River, not
to mention lesser streams that also contribute to the Sacramento
River. Los Angeles, in its desiccated basin, craves that water, and
gets that water, although it has to travel as much as five hundred

since he was a college basketball player who became the medical doctor for Princeton football, basketball, and baseball teams, and for United States Olympic teams as well. Born in 1895, he grew up in the age of the amateur athlete, never developed much interest in the professional-commercial complex, and may never have heard anyone say, "Time-out on the floor." If he had, and after the significance of it sank in, I think I would have heard an explosion.

Time-outs of all kinds have cumulatively damaged the dramatic structure of basketball and other sports. First, long ago, they replaced therapy with strategy, providing a number of opportunities for coaches to intervene, set ad hoc plays and defensive moves, and take a little more than something of the game away from the players. All that in itself was not especially harmful; and the number of time-outs was limited to a reasonable extent by the rules of the game. Now with the laser concentration of television, sport is inextricably related to marketing, and we have "time-out on the floor." No less an advertising medium than Google, it has doubled the intrusions and stiffened the entertainment. Time-outs in superabundance violate the spirit of the game. They turn coaches into puppeteers and players into puppets. Coaches call time-out to kill momentum, and with it kill the drama. "Time-out on the floor." Now watch and covet as I climb Pikes Peak in a Jaguar. Remember that you also need an F-150. Ford tough. Boom!

Time-out on the floor occurs every four minutes in a college basketball game, distending the event with thirty-two extra minutes of advertising. Enriched in clipboard time, coaches don't need to waste their own allotment of time-out calls, relying on "the floor" to serve the purpose. Their own time-outs accumulate like driftwood in an eddy, and the eddy becomes the finish, the climax of a close game. While clipboards flash and the game clock stutters forward, while players stand and stand and stand around their coaches, while Pikes Peak is ascended once again and you are told to see your doctor about side effects that could kill you, nothing happens on the court. The N.C.A.A. insists that this be a possibility in all college games, not just Duke versus Kentucky in behalf of General Motors. The N.C.A.A. has decreed that all college games be invaded by time-outs on the floor, whether or not the game is being broadcast.

If there is one chance in a million that a miracle will save a team that is down by three possessions with thirty-seven seconds to go, the coach will use a saved-up time-out. At the ends of games, close ones and not, real time will reach for midnight while the game clock seems paralyzed. Time-out on the floor is the older brother of pro football's two-minute warning, trapper of audiences in a web of advertising when audiences are least likely to get away.

I once intended to research this subject and do a potent brief aimed at reform, but these notes are brief enough.

Outcrops of Washington Road

Richard Steiner was a Princeton Township police officer, and became chief. He was short and compact, not especially athletic. His voice was quiet and soft but never retreating. He had been the president of our class at Princeton High School, and he grew up at Tusculum, on Cherry Hill Road. His father was the caretaker there, of the preserved estate of John Witherspoon, a Presbyterian minister from Paisley, Renfrewshire, Scotland, who—before, during, and after the American Revolution—was president of the college that is now Princeton University. After Nassau Street, which separates the Princeton municipality from the Princeton campus, the town's two principal thoroughfares are Witherspoon Street and Washington Road.

In 1963, when I was thirty-two years old, I was barrelling down Washington Road on my way to a commuter train when I was intersected by a car emerging from a side street called Faculty Road. Perhaps in part as a result, a traffic light is there now, but then there was just a stop sign. From a fair distance, I had seen the car, down on the right, waiting for a chance to turn left, and it kept on waiting until I was a few feet from the intersection, when it suddenly jumped out in front of me. Too late for evasive action—my skid marks did not even swerve—I hit the rear half of the car, totalling it and mine. I got out, walked a few feet to the base of a rock outcrop, sat down, and tried to collect my thoughts.

Police arrived, and talked to the other driver, who was unhurt. One officer came to me, crouched beside me, and asked if I was injured. Dick Steiner.

"Hello, Dick. I'm fine. I'm just getting my thoughts together."

Dick said, "You know—it's phenomenal. It happens fairly often. People walk away from an accident like that, say they're O.K., and feeling fine, and a few minutes later they fall over dead."

The outcrops and roadcuts on Washington Road close to Faculty Road are Stockton sandstone. In the eighteenth century, there were small quarries close by. A number of the college's first buildings—Nassau Hall, Stanhope Hall—are made of Stockton sandstone. I did not grow up aware of this but came to know it in my forties after I undertook to spend what turned out to be twenty years writing about geology. Since my early teens, though, I had been aware of a long-unquarried quarry off Washington Road, which Princeton police used as a pistol range. I had gone into it with Dr. William LeGrand Tucker, the minister of the Second Presbyterian Church, who also used it as a pistol range, and who taught me how to fire a .45. This narrow quarry, open to grade at its western end, was cut like a box canyon, deep between high walls of sandstone. Dr. Tucker lifted his .45, held it at arm's length, and fired at a target in the closed end. He handed me the gun. Today, in shoulder rehab, I lift three-pound weights at arms' length in a nonagenarian effort to keep on fly casting. At arm's length, that .45 seemed to weigh twenty pounds. Squeeze. Ka-BOOM! After the two-hundred-mulepower kick, I ended up two townships west. Or thought I did.

In the nineteen-eighties and nineteen-nineties, when my geology books were coming out, there were occasional photo shoots, set up by various media planning reviews. One photographer, arriving in Princeton, scouted scenes around the campus and then called to ask me if I would meet him on Washington Road, near Faculty Road, where I could stand on a sidewalk against a wall of rock that would—to a fare-thee-well—suggest geology. I met him there, and he started clicking the hundreds of pictures from which an editor would choose one. He was wearing a leather jacket and shades. Click. Blue jeans. Click. Click. Beard. Click. Click. Click. The camera was a small 35. After ten or fifteen minutes, a police car suddenly came out of Faculty Road, its tires squealing, and stopped with two wheels up on the Washington Road curb. Two cops sprang out, hands at holsters. Someone in a passing car had glanced at me and the photographer and had notified the police that a man up against a rock outcrop was being mugged at gunpoint, which, in a way, I was.

Blind Skier

Readers of William Shurtleff and Akiko Aoyagi's unpublished manuscript "History of Soybeans and Soyfoods, 1100 B.C. to the 1980s" may recall their account of an "early and very popular soymilk infant formula" called Mull-Soy. "In 1934, while director of allergy research for the Borden Company, Dr. Julius F. Muller developed a soymilk for his own child, who was highly allergic to dairy milk. Muller formed his own company, Muller Laboratories in Baltimore, introduced Mull-Soy commercially in early 1936, and promoted it by his own efforts."

His child's name was Edward. In the nineteen-forties, the family moved to 35 Westcott Road in Princeton, New Jersey, and at Princeton High School Ed and I, aged fourteen, were alphabetically assigned to adjacent desks in homeroom. He was legally blind. He wore glasses with lenses half an inch thick. He held a printed page almost against them in order to read anything. Now and again, I helped him. His father's synthetic milk had helped save the eyesight of other children but not Ed's.

Ed was a talented pianist even then. His sense of humor was off the scale. He soaked up and emanated gossip. From that first September on, he was part of the group I hung out with in high school—Louise Stoll, Carol Brock, Howland Swift, Dick Clothier, Peggy Fales, Arne Booth, Bob Delsasso, Ed Muller—and increas-

ingly I read things to him: books we were assigned in class, pieces I
had written, miscellaneous stuff. The Mullers had a summer house
in Westport, New York, on Lake Champlain. They would invite
me to come over there at the end of August—after the season at
Keewaydin, the canoe-tripping camp I went to, in Vermont. Ed
had two brothers—Dick and Jim—and the four of us drove up to
Montreal (Dick was old enough to drive) in the family convertible.
But mostly Ed and I swam in the lake and sat on the dock with a
book. I read *The Scarlet Letter* to him, *The Sun Also Rises*, a scattered
list. Something close to forty years would go by before I came to
realize the extent to which reading those books and pieces aloud to
Ed Muller would help the development of the writer I hoped to be.

For some years his day job was accompanist at the Martha Gra-
Ed went to Oberlin College and on from Oberlin to the Juilliard School at Lincoln Center. He became a concert pianist and
for some years his day job was accompanist at the Martha Graham Dance Company and the Martha Graham Studio Theater.
I saw little of him then, and nothing at all after he moved to
Arizona, was trained as a psychologist, established a practice, and
became a blind skier. We did stay in touch, though, by letter, then
e-mail, and infrequent phone calls. In high school, he had shown
no interest whatever in any form of athleticism, and none in his
Manhattan years. But now he was schussbooming downhill on
Rocky Mountain snow with a sign on his chest: BLIND SKIER. He
died of something else in 2007.

For some twenty-five years, I have read the second drafts of
my pieces of writing to Gordon Gund at his office in Princeton.
He is a fishing companion, and he is also blind. The Foundation
Fighting Blindness—established by Gordon, his wife, Lulie, and
others—is, as its website claims, "the world's leading private funder
of retinal disease research." The help he gives me is not in the

hope that something may happen twenty years hence but with the sound and sense of what is there and not there now. As I have said of him before, he does not miss a word. Like my wife, Yolanda, he is a world-class listener in a world in which so few people listen. He is also an amazing fly caster—totally blind—sending his shooting head far across rivers then touching the current with the tip of the rod, sensing drift and when to mend and when to start the retrieve. He is an athlete, obviously, was an ice-hockey player in college. Harvard. He was a pilot of light aircraft until he lost his sight in his thirties to retinitis pigmentosa. He is eighty-three years old at this writing. For a while each winter, he is in Colorado, where he goes downhill on Rocky Mountain snow wearing a blaze-orange vest with big black letters: BLIND SKIER.

Writing About Science

For two semesters a few years apart, Jeremy Bernstein was a visiting professor in the journalism program at Princeton, and both times he was assigned to an office next to mine. Jeremy was not just a *New Yorker* staff writer and author of pieces on high-altitude climbing and profiles of eminent scientists. He was also a theoretical physicist. He believed that a writer not trained in science had no business writing about science. Pal that he was, he nonetheless had no discernible reticence when it came to sounding this theme.

C. P. Snow, novelist, physical chemist, in his essay "The Two Cultures" (1959), described with some dismay the moat that separates the scientific from the literary, the numerate from the innumerate, the lab from the landscape. If you are among the innumerate, and you undertake to write about science, you ignore Jeremy, but you develop criteria before you cross the moat and attempt to obtain from the scientific culture material to take back to the other side.

I once planned to write a book on this subject and dedicate it to Jeremy, but a few primary points are as much as I ever assembled.

For example, you want the finished piece not only to impress, educate, and even entertain a general readership but also to be acceptable to the category of scientists about whom you are writing. If the subject is fluvial geomorphology, the result should seem right and sound to fluvial geomorphologists. This involves—for me, anyway—breaking the fundamental rule of journalism that you never show a manuscript to the subject. I have always adhered to that rule with the consistent exception of pieces about science. It has not been my purpose to write for a scientific audience, but my purpose would be defeated if my work were not acceptable to scientists. I showed Ted Taylor the first draft of *The Curve of Binding Energy* and every iteration thereafter through more drafts, galleys, and page proofs. Ted was a theoretical physicist, a designer of nuclear bombs very large and very small, and *The Curve of Binding Energy* was about his concern that weapons-grade nuclear material in the possession of private industry was inadequately protected. The piece involved discussions of neutron scattering, transuranium elements, fission, fusion, production reactors, isotopic enrichment, and two ways to achieve a critical mass—not the sort of thing I learned in English 404.

I also knew nothing back then of plate theory, geophysical hot spots, and the ophiolitic sequence, in part because no one else did. The seminal papers of the plate-tectonics revolution were written in a decade that began in 1959, six years after I finished college. All I knew about the science then was from a geomorphology course I had in high school. In 1978, when I undertook to write about the geosciences, I had no idea that I was getting into something that would take me twenty years. That's a lot of time on the other side of the moat. Each of my mentoring scientists read the pertinent manuscript and went over it with me before publication. At the U.S. Geological Survey, in Reston, Virginia, the conodont paleontologist Anita Harris read passages aloud to the people in her lab, while I sat there dumbfounded by this delightful perversion of protocol. I was also remembering Anita in the Delaware Water Gap when I asked her—as we walked upsection from Silurian quartzite to Devonian sandstone—how often she had been accompanied on her field trips by people like me. She said, "I haven't worked on this level in I don't know when." David Love, in Laramie, and also of the U.S.G.S., set right the details of his native Wyoming, but—while not suggesting the redaction of anything—recused himself from the new tectonics. He had seen the future and at that point it was not his.

Jeremy might have been right. Jeremy might have been wrong. But that is pretty much where I would have begun the book on writing about science dedicated to him, and a closely following passage would have suggested that an especially useful device in writing about science is to describe children learning the subject. Judy Moores, wife of the tectonicist Eldridge Moores, taught elementary plate tectonics to children in Davis, California, where Eldridge was a professor at U.C. Davis. Judy held her hands out toward the children, palms down, thumbs tucked under, index fingers pressed together side by side, and she slid the left hand forward, the right hand backward as she described a strike-slip fault, specifically a right-lateral strike-slip fault, the San Andreas Fault. Starting afresh, she held out her hands palms down, index fingers together, and slowly drew her hands apart—two plates separating with bilateral symmetry, the Mid-Atlantic Ridge, the East Pacific Rise. She then turned one hand, and shoved it under the other—subduction, the Mariana Trench, the Aleutian Trench. And finally she put her hands together as at the beginning, but jammed them against each other so that they buckled and formed an inverted V—plate-to-plate collision, India collides with Asia.

In writing about science, one is always aware that the reader may know a good deal more about the science than the writer does, or a good deal less, and that both categories of reader are always going to be there, in some ratio or other. So, as I'm suggesting, you look for ways to put things that would inform the unknowledgeable while not irritating the knowledgeable. This is not an easy matter, but you can find a way. When Ted Taylor was growing up in Mexico, he had a chemistry set, he listened to classical music, and he played billiards. How these facts and high-school experience related to the particle physicist he would become are described in two passages from *The Curve of Binding Energy*, which also cover the problem of how to deal with something as essential to your story as the periodic table of the elements without anesthetizing that portion of your readership that knows it all before opening your book.

In the afternoons after school, for a number of years, Ted played billiards almost every day, averaging about ten hours of billiards a week. He was, among his friends, exceptionally skillful. He knew nothing of particle physics—of capture

cross-sections and neutron scattering, of infinite reflectors
and fast-neutron-induced fission chain reactions—but in a
sense he was beginning to learn it, because he understood
empirically the behavior of the interacting balls on the table,
and the nature of their elastic collisions, all within the con-
fining framework of the reflector cushions. "It was a game
of skill, dealing with predictable situations—an exact game.
The reason it appealed to me was probably the same reason
physics appeals to me. I like to be able to predict what will
happen and have it come out that way. If you play billiards a
lot, you find you can have a great deal of control over what
happens. You can get all kinds of things to happen. I have
thought of billiard balls as the examples in physics as long
as I can remember—as examples of types of collisions from
Newton's mechanics to atomic particles. The balls made a
satisfying click if they were new and expensive. Downtown,
they were new and expensive. It was a treat to go downtown.
You could try a twelve-cushion shot there."

———————

In the fall of 1941, Ted Taylor went to Exeter, for one year of
additional schooling, and in the New Hampshire winter he
knew frozen ponds and rivers for the first time. He learned
to skate. The feel of it energized him in the way that someone
else his age might have been excited by a first chance to drive
a car. He would skate alone in the afternoons ten miles up
the Exeter River, through boggy woods, watching through ice
as clear as window glass the rocks and pine needles on the bed
of the river. He was taking "Modern Physics" under Elbert P.

Little, a teacher of such ability that old Exonians thirty and forty years away from Exeter still remember him with particular and affectionate awe. He gave Ted a D, a flat and final D, and even in the winter term Ted could see that D was his status, and that it was unlikely to rise. He barely noticed, because with his D he was getting a look for the first time—and a vividly clear one—at what he would call "submicroscopic solar systems," and he found that they had for him enormous appeal. One proton with an electron (about eighteen hundred and fifty times lighter) orbiting around it—hydrogen. One proton and one neutron together in a nucleus with an electron orbiting around it—heavy hydrogen (deuterium). Two protons and a number of neutrons with two electrons orbiting around them—helium. Three protons, some neutrons, three whirling electrons—lithium. One at a time, add a proton and an electron, and each element became another. Four protons, four electrons—beryllium. Five—boron. Six—carbon. Seven—nitrogen . . . Seventy—ytterbium . . . Seventy-eight—platinum. Seventy-nine protons—gold. Eighty protons—mercury (eighty protons massed together with anywhere from ninety-nine to a hundred and twenty-six neutrons into a body around which orbited eighty electrons, whose negative charges exactly balanced the eighty positive charges of the protons). Eighty-one protons—thallium. Eighty-two protons—lead. Bismuth. Polonium. Astatine. Radon. Francium. Radium. Actinium. Ninety protons— thorium. Ninety-one protons—protactinium. Neutrons had no charge and were neither attracted nor repelled by electrical forces and were thus the particles that could most easily be taken out of one atom and shot into the nucleus of another. Ninety-two protons, ninety-two electrons, a gross (more or less) of neutrons—uranium. The list, at the time, stopped there, having included everything that was found in nature. The transuranium elements were just beginning to be discovered and were not known in Exeter. Out on the river, skating, he pondered the root simplicity that all things he had ever seen—wood and water, bread and candle wax—were made of neutrons, protons, and electrons, separated by space. He tried to imagine what it would be like to live on an electron. What would the nucleus look like as a sun? There were a sextillion protons, a sextillion electrons, and a sextillion neutrons in one dead leaf on the bottom of the river. There was an island universe in a drop of water. His imagination outgrew his chemistry lab in Mexico City. He decided that he wanted to be a physicist.

No letter that ever came to me from a reader can quite match one, on stationery of the Memorial Sloan-Kettering Cancer Center, in New York, from Dr. Lewis Thomas, its president. He was the author of regular essays in *The New England Journal of Medicine* that were collected as books that reached the top of the *New York Times* best-seller list—*The Lives of a Cell*, *The Medusa and the Snail*, *The Youngest Science*. He was Lewis Thomas and he was telling me that he liked something that I had written about science. I did not need a higher prize. He also told me about an experience he had in the nineteen-thirties when he was an undergraduate at Princeton. He had gone to the campus medical center to report that he was dying. That, at least, was his diagnosis and he had come to the McCosh Infirmary to confirm it. My father, the physician who examined him, listened to his lungs and heart, and shaped a diagnosis of his own. He said, "Thomas, you are hung over. Go back to your room and sleep it off."

Meredith Willson

For some years, back in the old century, I carried in my head a set of facts directed toward a profile of Meredith Willson—the Meredith Willson from Davenport, Iowa, on the Mississippi River; the Meredith Willson trained in music and an obscure employee of CBS; the Meredith Willson who wrote just one musical play. He wrote all of it—book, lyrics, music—in a feat without parallel on Broadway. In exuberant homage to his home town, he stage-named it "River City," and presented its story with a big parade led by seventy-six trombones. As a composer, Willson was so prestidigitational that the trombone march and one of the love songs ("Goodnight My Someone") were so different in texture and tempo that you blinked once or twice before realizing that they were the same tune. And Willson went back to CBS for the rest of his days, leaving behind him *The Music Man*.

Nonfiction stories never turn out exactly as they seemed in concept, some not even close. So it would have been with Meredith Willson. How that conceptual cloud took form I can't begin to remember, but as a piece of factual writing it would have, well, evolved. Willson was born and grew up in Mason City, Iowa, two hundred miles from Davenport and the Mississippi River.

He went to Frank Damrosch's Institute of Musical Art, in New
York, which eventually became the Juilliard School of Music.
For many years, he lived in Brentwood, California (read Hollywood), where he worked on shows with Fred Astaire, Ginger
Rogers, Frank Sinatra, Tallulah Bankhead, George Burns, Gra-
cie Allen, Jack Benny, Bing Crosby. He wrote, in all, four musical plays, including *The Unsinkable Molly Brown*, which ran on
Broadway for five-hundred-and-thirty-two performances. The list
of individuals who have written the book, lyrics, and score of
musical plays is a long one. Willson was a flautist, playing both
flute and piccolo. He was in John Philip Sousa's band. Ditto the
New York Philharmonic—Arturo Toscanini, maestro. Willson
did various shows for NBC as well as CBS. With Charlie Chaplin,
he co-wrote the score of Chaplin's film *The Great Dictator*. He
wrote two symphonies and three autobiographies, including *Eggs
I Have Laid* (Holt, 1955).

The Impostor Syndrome

When I was a child hanging around my father and Princeton
athletes, I had no sense whatever that any of them felt that they
were impostors, frauds, and unworthy of being at Princeton. I
thought they were straight off Mount Olympus, but I was eight
years old. Ten years later, when I was a student at Princeton myself
and forming friendships with some remarkable athletes, I never
met one who thought he did not belong in his sport or in the
college, but that was seven decades ago. Well into the twenty-first

century, at a meeting of the Princeton men's lacrosse team—a forum, sort of, with coaches, faculty, deans, and so on—I was startled to hear one player say that he and most, if not all, of the others were afflicted with impostor syndrome. They felt they had been admitted to Princeton not so much because they were good students but because they were also skilled lacrosse players, and in their own view were impostors, frauds, second-class citizens. One of my college roommates won football's Heisman Trophy, and for the rest of his life said that what had mattered to him most was the school he belonged to, and the Heisman Trophy was just "an interesting, external part of the picture." This was Dick Kazmaier. Although he majored in psychology, he did not even know what the impostor syndrome was, because the term did not come along for another twenty-seven years.

In 2014, Olivia Robbins, a student in my writing class, wrote about the "impostor syndrome," saying that most Princeton students have it—athletes and not. They feel that they don't belong in such a place, that everybody else is superior in intelligence, et cetera, et cetera, and many another cetera. Someday, this might be a good subject for me, I thought. But I was more than intimidated by the Clance Impostor Phenomenon Scale and where I might register upon it.

Sloop to Gibraltar

I thought once of writing about what happens to some books. I had in mind my own. A grizzly ate one—in a trapper's cabin

on a Yukon tributary a couple of hundred miles northeast of
Fairbanks—or at least destroyed it, tore it apart, and whole chap-
ters were missing. The book, *Coming into the Country*, was in some
measure about the grizzly, and the trapper figured prominently
in it, too. I sent him another copy, with an inscription noting
that I was glad he had not been in the cabin when the bear
broke in.

Another trapper, in a neighboring drainage, fell out of his canoe in high water and drowned. His inscribed copy of the same
book ended up on Amazon.com. A dozen books, inscribed pri-
vately across fifteen years to my editor Robert Bingham, ended up
in the same public receptacle. Bob Bingham died young, of brain
cancer, and his books were bought by a dealer. Tough to tender,
green to purple, write what you will in a private inscription. It will
end up on Amazon.

"To my mother and father, without whom . . ." $19.50.

Chasing down inscriptions that come to odd light and book
copies with surprising fates was not a great idea for a piece of writing
and I would have realized that at a much earlier date were it not for
a letter, postmarked somewhere in Florida, that came to me in the
nineteen-nineties. I have lost it somehow, and can't remember the
name of the young man who wrote to me, or of his mother, or of his
crewman, but I could never forget the story he told me. Somebody
in Switzerland had bought a sloop in Florida. The guy who wrote
the letter had been hired to sail the sloop across the Atlantic and
deliver it in Gibraltar. With a friend as crewman, he was ready to
cast off from Fort Lauderdale when his mother came to say good-
bye. She had a going-away present for him, for both of them, a copy
of *Looking for a Ship*.

The book had been published recently and had by far the most complicated structure of any book I had written or would write thereafter. The structure looked like this:

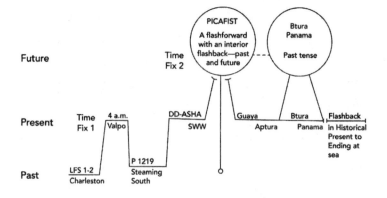

Try sailing that across the Atlantic. Its oddity was the result of attempts to get certain effects, nearly all involving Paul McHenry Washburn, captain of the S.S. Stella Lykes, U.S. Merchant Marine. In 1988, when I went to the Masters, Mates & Pilots union hall in Charleston, South Carolina, with Andy Chase, a second mate looking for a ship, Andy, of course, had no idea what ship—if any—he would get. If a job arose, we meant to ask the shipping company if I could go along—as a P.A.C., Person in Addition to Crew—for the purpose of writing about the Merchant Marine, and that was a long shot, too. In other words, the whole approach was completely random; and what should come steaming toward Charleston with a second mate getting off there? The S.S. Stella Lykes. Run: the west coast of South America.

Six weeks, six countries, three stowaways, and a few dozen

pirates later, I had come to regard being on Captain Washburn's
ship as a piece of luck comparable to playing a complete round
of his favorite game (golf) in eighteen strokes. He epitomized
the Merchant Marine. He had learned from the old skippers, as
old skippers of the future would learn from him. He was aloof,
commanding, understanding, sympathetic, and utterly adroit in
the skills of his demanding profession. His sense of humor could
cut fog. About some topics he was confessedly vitriolic, but from
the engine room to the bridge the ship was running on respect
for him.

In the book that I later wrote is this passage: "When Captain
Washburn looks landward from the bridge of his ship, he will
readily say, 'I would rather be here for the worst that could be here
than over there for the best that could be there . . . I once thought
I was going to college and be a history teacher, but I have never
been able to concentrate on anything else but this . . . By the end
of 1945, I had passed the point of no return. I was in the soup now
good. Anything adverse that came up, this was my safety blanket:
"Hey, I can get a ship." If I made plans and they went wrong, I
was gone—looking for a ship.'"

Something adverse that came up was the Washington Redskins' performance against the Philadelphia Eagles on the twenty-
seventh of October, 1946. Captain Washburn's home was in the
District of Columbia, and the Redskins were more important to
him than any other group of people on land. He had developed
an affectionate and protective sympathy for the Redskins after
the Chicago Bears beat them 73–0 in their fourth Washington
season. Washburn, who was at that game, had been following
the team even before they came to Washington. He remembered

them as the Boston Redskins. He remembered many of them as Duluth Eskimos. And now, on this significant Sunday in 1946, the Redskins led the Eagles 24–0 at the half. The final score was Philadelphia 28, Washington 24.

"I couldn't handle defeat like that," he said. "I can't now. I picked an argument with my wife. I remember saying, 'Listen, woman, I don't have to listen to this. I can go back to sea.' She said, 'Listen, jackass, if you go back to sea, if you come back to this house it will be so empty it will look like no one ever lived in it.' In those days, you didn't wave any red flags or throw gauntlets in front of the kid. November 7th, I was fireman and water tender on a ship out of Baltimore leaving for Poland."

And forty-two years later, in pre-dawn darkness on the bridge of the Stella Lykes, he was frustrated anew as he approached Valparaiso and tried and tried again to radio the port. "So much for moving ships at this hour in the morning," the captain said. "The port isn't even awake yet. When Ethan Allen was expiring, people said to him, 'Ethan, the angels expect you,' and Ethan said, 'God damn them. Let them wait.' Then he expired."

The complete resonance of the captain's parable passed above the head of the Person in Addition to Crew. In the dark, the captain paced back and forth across the wheelhouse. Andy was also a bridge pacer. Andy and the captain had long since developed a collision-avoidance system. "I don't stay in one place," the captain said. "I never did. I don't stay in one place even when I'm *in* one place. Give 'em a moving target."

The sloop from Fort Lauderdale was somewhere west of the Azores when the gift copy of *Looking for a Ship* went to the

bottom of the ocean, fourteen thousand feet down, where it settled on the abyssal plain, the sloop with it. According to the letter
from the young skipper, the crossing had gone smoothly for something like twenty-five hundred miles, and he and his crewman
had read the book. Then a great storm arose, mountainous seas,
and the sloop was destroyed. It had a Zodiac raft, and the two
young men escaped on it. They had also been able to send out
an SOS.

For some time, they clung to the raft, and then, miraculously,
a merchant ship appeared through the stinging rain and came
over the raging seas to rescue them. Flying the American flag, it
was a Ro/Ro (roll-on, roll-off) and what it had aboard to roll off
were U.S. Army tanks on their way to the Gulf War. At that time,
about twenty-three thousand six hundred merchant ships were on
the world's oceans, while the size of the U.S. merchant fleet was
down to six hundred and dropping. Of those twenty-three thousand ships, this one was closest to the sunken sloop. The skipper
of the Ro/Ro was waiting for the two men as they were hauled up
the side and through a bunker port. Welcome aboard, guys. This
is Captain Washburn.

When they neared Gibraltar, there was no way he was going
to let them off. To dock in Gibraltar would have cost him five
thousand dollars. He had been talking to them nonstop since he
picked them up, and he went on talking to them as the Ro/Ro
went through the Mediterranean. Without doubt, they heard
at least three times about each of the old skippers with whom
Washburn had sailed when he was young, and on whose seaman-
ship he had modelled his own: Leadline Dunn, Terrible Terry
Harmon, Dirty Shirt George Price, Rebel Frazier, Clean Shirt

George Price, Herbert P. High Pressure Erwin. Captain Washburn had saved the young men's lives, and now he was talking them to death.

He let them off in Port Said.

The Valley

I am happy to say that I never took up a promising piece called "The Valley." I achieved this ambiguously negative and positive attitude in 2016. The idea had come to me, and even the title, on a frozen lake in northernmost Maine in 1984. In a light plane equipped with skis, I was flying from lake to lake with a warden pilot named John McPhee (yes), who was checking the licenses of people fishing through the ice. On the small lake—near the Canadian border, which is also the St. John River—were two quite separate ice-fishing shacks, and while the warden lingered at the first one I walked on toward the other.

People who live on or near the St. John refer to their world as the Valley. Some are Americans, some are Canadians, but they call themselves and think of themselves as people of the Valley. They have more in common with one another than they do with the people elsewhere in their own countries. On the shelves of an American general store, you would see Mélasse Qualité Fantaisie, Pure de la Barbade, Scott tissue, Sirop d'Érable Pur, and Ivory liquid detergent. As I walked across the snow-covered ice, a kid came out of the fishing shack and walked toward me. He appeared to be teen-aged, an American high-school student, evidently alone there and glad to have some company. With a big welcoming smile, he said to me, "Parlez-vous français?"

Along the Rio Grande in southern Texas, people on both sides of the river refer to the place where they live as the Valley. What I thought of writing, under that singular title, was a composition of alternating parts from the American-Mexican and American-Canadian milieus. I let thirty years go by while I mused about it, then along came Donald Trump with his cockamamie wall, and instead of writing "The Valley" I found myself scribbling incoherent abstracts like "Trumpty Dumpty sat on a wall" and "Oh, say, can you see what my base sees in me?"

December 19, 1943

In Sunday school, in the fall of the year when I was twelve years old, I was told that I would be ushering and passing a collection plate at the Christmas pageant, an annual living crèche in the First Presbyterian Church of Princeton. I hated Sunday school. I resented having to attend. I learned nothing. I went to school Monday through Friday and that was enough. I was a spiritual wasteland, then as now. But I shrugged and didn't think about the pageant until the day was nigh and Julian Boyd—who was thirteen, and did not go to Sunday school—told me about adventures he was having skating up the Millstone River, and asked me to come with him on, as it happened, the afternoon of the Christmas pageant. With no hesitation, I said I would.

My mother saw this in a different light. She said, "You are not going skating with Julian. You are ushering at the Christmas pageant."

I pointed out that I was just one of several ushers.

Her next remark was identical to the first one.

John Graham, twelve years old, had been invited by Julian to skate up the Millstone on the same afternoon. John was in no way burdened by religion, and planned to go. Charlie Howard, twelve, had already skated up the river on the ice with Julian, and would be coming along this time, too.

My mother was—in a word she liked—adamant. I howled and moaned and griped and begged. Adamant.

The afternoon came, and by now you may have guessed where I was. In the church. Passing the plate. Mad as hell. Obedient.

John Graham had come down with a severe cold, and stayed at home in bed.

Julian and Charlie died at an isolated place called the Sheep Wash, where the current of the Millstone sped up and the ice as a result was thin. Next day, their bodies were collected off the bottom with grappling hooks. Each boy's arms were stiff, and reaching forward, straight out from the shoulders. They had gone into the water through the thin ice, then clung to stronger ice closer to the edge of the river, but had not been able to climb out. Their arms reached over the ice, supporting them, until the cold killed them.

Their small coffins were placed side by side in the crossing under the choir loft in the Princeton University Chapel. Helen Howard, Charlie's mother, was nearby, with Charlie's father, Stanley Howard, a professor of economics; as was Grace Boyd, Julian's mother, with her younger son, Kenneth, and her husband, Julian Boyd, editor of the papers of Thomas Jefferson. This was the second such funeral for the Boyds, who had lost a daughter some years before.

I did not know Charlie Howard well, and the impact of his death stopped there. Not so with Julian, whose future has remained beside me through all my extending past. That is to say, where would he have been, and doing what, when? From time to time across the decades, I have thought of writing something, tracing parallel to mine the life he would have lived, might have lived. A chronology, a chronicle, a lost C.V. But such, of course, from the first imagined day, is fiction. Actually, I have to try not to think about him, because I see those arms reaching forward, grasping nothing.

The Dutch Ship Tyger

The Tiger, or Tyger, a merchant vessel from the Netherlands, crossed the Atlantic in 1613. The skipper's name was Adriaen Block and the ship's mission was to fill up with furs obtained from American tribes. Across recent decades, scholars on both sides of the Atlantic have parsed its story to a fare-thee-well, but records are very limited and much of the Tyger's story, while long thought to be true, is based on probability and conjecture. In repeating it here, I have been mindful of scholars' facts and suppositions while preserving the story as I learned it. Furs collected, the Dutch ship was anchored in the Hudson River at Manhattan when it caught fire and burned to the waterline, and the crew were as stranded as they would have been had the island beside them been in Micronesia. After beaching the Tyger and removing some materials, the crew went ashore, marooned.

I first heard about the Tyger from Bob VanDeventer, in 1962, when he was working for the Port of New York Authority, on Eighth Avenue, and I at *Time: The Weekly Newsmagazine*, on Sixth. We had been friends and teammates in high school. He was now an inchoate writer of fiction and I the other way around. At lunch one day in Greenwich Village, I told him that I had written to *The New Yorker* asking to become one of their contributors, and had received a response inviting me to submit some sample writing at the length of the pieces in *The New Yorker*'s section called The Talk of the Town.

I have long meant to amplify this account as part of an anti-cautionary tale for young writers, as a chronicle of rejection as a curable disease, and as a reminder that most writers grow slowly over time, but so far I've preferred just to tell it to them. In short, I was in high school when I decided that what I wanted to do in life was write for *The New Yorker*, in college when I first sent a manuscript to the magazine, and in college when I filed away that first rejection slip and the second and the sixteenth, then on through my twenties and into my thirties, when the whole of that collection of rejection slips could have papered a wall.

The *New Yorker* person who wrote back to me in 1962 was Leo Hofeller, whose title was executive editor. I sent him a couple of pieces I don't remember, and a piece on an urban farmer who was growing sweet corn in a vacant lot on Avenue C, but the one I had the most hope for was the Dutch ship. It was such a New York story. In my mind's eye, I could see it under *The New Yorker*'s distinct Rea Irvin typeface. As the story unfolded, Adriaen Block and his crew built log cabins, about where the twin towers of the World Trade Center would be built. They lived in the cabins through the winter of 1614 and were the first European residents of Manhattan. They busied themselves building a small caravel, and in the spring went off to hunt for a ship to take them home. They sailed up the East River into Long Island Sound, and beyond Montauk Point they saw in the ocean—freestanding and imposing—the island that they named for Adriaen Block. Looking for a way home, they found it, probably on a merchant ship that happened upon them and picked them up.

In 1916, sandhogs tunneling a subway line under Greenwich and Dey Streets—on the seventeenth-century shoreline of Manhattan—encountered the bow of an ancient ship sticking out from one side. They were about to destroy it when their history-minded foreman told them to cut it off and keep those eight and a half feet whole. Today, that piece is in the Museum of the City of New York. Long thought to have been the prow of the Tyger, it is now ascribed to a somewhat later era. The rest of the ship was not removed and was probably destroyed in the nineteen-sixties, during the excavation for the Twin Towers. In 1962, meanwhile, preparing my sample Talk piece for Leo Hofeller, I visited the museum, on Fifth Avenue at 103rd Street, and I went to Brooklyn to interview James Kelly, the sandhog foreman who had caused the nautical artifact to be preserved. Amiable, informative, delightful, he was no longer digging subways, having become an official historian of the City of Brooklyn.

A couple of weeks after I sent in those sample Talk pieces, a note came from Hofeller. He would like to talk. Could I come to 25 West Forty-third Street at a certain time on a certain day. Could I! I found his office, on the nineteenth floor. On his desk were my sample pieces and the *Daily Racing Form*. He was colloquial, a little gruff. He said, "These pieces are pretty good." He paused, and looked at me in a way suggesting that he had placed a bet and was feeling bettor's remorse. Then he said, "Now don't misunderstand me. I said 'pretty good.' I did not say 'very good.'" That the magazine had no intention of buying any of those sample pieces was clear without articulation, but Hofeller did finish off the meeting by suggesting that as time went along I might suggest to the magazine longer projects that I might do.

About then Harold Hayes, an editor at *Esquire*, wrote to me at *Time* and asked if I would like to freelance a piece for *Esquire*, and, if so, we could talk about it over lunch. I had never met him, but he had apparently read a couple of my *Time* cover stories, probably the ones on Jackie Gleason and Sophia Loren. In Princeton, New Jersey, my home town, I had bought some property and was planning to build a house, and was therefore moonlighting feverishly to help pay for it. As a writer at *Time*, you could freelance not only for other Time Inc. publications but also for sections of *Time* itself other than your own. I was the writer of the Show Business section. So I reviewed books at a nervous clip. The extra pay was good. For Time-Life Books, I anonymously revised a manuscript that had made them unhappy. And I went to lunch with Harold Hayes.

I told him that I had once suited up to play basketball for the University of Cambridge against Her Majesty's Royal Fusiliers in the central courtyard of the Tower of London, a venue that was shifted at the last moment because a lorry backed into and broke down one of the baskets. I had been thinking of writing the story on a freelance basis for some time. Now, said Hayes, happily commissioning the piece, but after I wrote it and sent it to him he rejected it. Depressed, thirty-one years old, I recklessly sent it to *Sports Illustrated* and *The New Yorker* simultaneously. A few weeks went by, another freelanced book review, and then my phone rang at *Time*. *The New Yorker* was buying the piece. Oh my God. Breathlessly, I went to the elevator and down to *Sports Illustrated* and called on Jack Tibby, an assistant managing editor, who coordinated outside submissions. I had not previously met him. I asked him to return the manuscript to me, and I said why. A large pile of manuscripts was on a corner of his desk. He said that actually *Sports Illustrated* was quite interested in the manuscript and he could not give it back to me. Hunting for it in the pile on his desk, he needed some minutes to find it. As he searched, he was murmuring something and it soon blossomed into a cloud of fury. How dared I—a Time Inc. writer—submit a piece to *The New Yorker*? He was going to see that this breach of loyalty was reported to Henry Luce and everybody else on the thirty-fourth floor, not to mention Otto Fuerbringer, the managing editor of *Time*. Above all, he would try to see to it that the sale to *The New Yorker* was blocked. Shell-shocked, I interrupted him. "Mr. Tibby," I blurted, "I beg you not to do that." I told him this was the most important moment of my professional life, that I had been trying to sell something to *The New Yorker* for fifteen years and everything had failed. "I beg you to give me that manuscript." He looked at me for a long moment, his face softened, and he handed me the story. I never heard of or from him again.

"Basketball and Beefeaters" ran in *The New Yorker* in March, 1963. It was in the category of reminiscence that *The New Yorker* called casuals, and was handled by the fiction department, fact notwithstanding. It gave me enormous pleasure but had no discernible effect on my future. Nobody was asking for more, so I wrote to Leo Hofeller and asked him for advice. Some days later, he responded, saying that I could send him a list of ideas for longer, factual pieces, including profiles. I sent him some, mentioning among them a possible profile on Bill Bradley. Days passed before I heard from him. He said to go ahead and try one of those pieces, "but not that basketball player; we just did a profile of a basketball player."

Bradley by now was in his third year at Princeton. I had watched him in his freshman season, in which he broke a record by making fifty-seven consecutive foul shots, and had since been present at all his home games. Everyone around Princeton basketball thought him as rare a person as a player, and so he would seem to me, for the canonical work ethic, the monastic and ecclesiastical work ethic, that resulted in scoring feats such as thirty-six points against Syracuse, forty-six against the University of Texas, and forty-seven against Wisconsin, a record for the Kentucky Invitational Tournament. Not to mention his commitment to teach Sunday School in the mornings after his Saturday-night games, even if they had been played at Harvard, Dartmouth, or Cornell. I knew this about him but had never met him, yet I decided that for the time being I was more interested in writing about him than in writing for *The New Yorker*. I wrote a letter to Leo Hofeller thanking him and saying that I hoped to be in touch with him at some future date but meanwhile I was going ahead with the basketball player for any publication that might show interest in the finished piece. I didn't stop there. Compulsively, unconsciously, I just kept writing that letter, trying to explain why I was going ahead anyway, trying to describe Bradley's way of playing basketball, his court sense, his array of shots, his no-look passes that seemed always to end up in the hands they were meant for. The length of the letter was five thousand words. After a time, and to my surprise, Hofeller replied. Despite what he had told me, he said, *The New Yorker* would like to read the piece when I had finished it, "no guarantees, of course." He added that what had interested the magazine most was the technical stuff.

That was in March, 1964. *The New Yorker* bought the piece in November, and Leo Hofeller again asked me to come to 25 West Forty-third Street. I had not really sensed that, while his title was executive editor, he was not an editor in the usual definition of the word. He dealt with would-bes and wannabes but not with pieces going to press. When the horses were running at Belmont Park, his hours in the office were said to be reduced. He told me this time that I was to forget absolutely everything he had ever said to me. I was about to enter a different dialogue. Then he walked me to the office of William Shawn. The profile was published in January, 1965, Shawn its editor. Some weeks later, around my thirty-fourth birthday, I was added to the list of *New Yorker* staff writers, actually a freelance arrangement with a "best efforts" con-tract, spectacularly brief. In those days, you just agreed to give your best efforts to *The New Yorker*.

Ray Brock

What do you have to be to be carried away by bullfighting and by Ernest Hemingway's descriptions of it? Immature comes to mind.

card, from the first spin of a cape to the last kill. We could afford *sol*, sometimes *sol y sombra*, never better. Looking around, we saw many faces that did not look Spanish. A lot, plainly, were American college kids, American male college kids. In fact, we recognized quite a few of them. One such moment has never faded in my mind's eye. An American college student, two years behind me at Princeton, whom I had known at home but not well, happened to be sitting near us, and after a dying bull hemorrhaged through its nostrils I saw that the kid was weeping. We did not see him again there. Three or four years later, he was training as a Navy pilot, flying a jet fighter off a carrier. He missed a landing, and the plane, right side up, went onto the water. He tried to open the canopy and get out, but the canopy was stuck shut and wouldn't budge. The plane filled with water. Sailors who observed it go down said he looked up at them, raised his hands past his head in the spreading gesture of helplessness, and shrugged.

In crowded barrooms, crowded cafés, we drank red wine that, like sangria, was set on the table in pitchers. If the person next to you shouted loudly enough, you could sometimes hear what was said. We hunted for scenes of relative quiet, and one night, in a room with well-spaced round tables, we sat opposite a man and a woman who seemed interested in who we might be and where from, and what, if anything, went on in our minds. If they were interested in us, the reverse was more than so, because they looked exactly like every picture we had ever seen of Mary Welsh Hemingway and Ernest Hemingway. They did not introduce themselves. If you had seen a *Look* magazine cover, a *Time* cover, a *Life* cover, there it was, across the table. Her blondness. His white beard. Her compactness. His heft. Her smile, and his. Their photogenic faces.

Could it be? Since 1923, he had been here many times. Why not this time? If he could drive to Paris while bullets were still flying, why not Pamplona while bulls were still running? This for him was a magnetic town, a place to beat the odds he was always beating. Of course, the man and woman at the barroom table could be fakes, impersonators, but this was early for that. By 2010, there were four hundred thousand Elvis Presleys extant, some of them women. And it was not unknown for passengers on airplanes to find themselves sitting next to Chairman Mao, especially in China, where at least one Mao Zedong was a woman.

Finally, I asked the white-bearded papa across the table point-blank to tell us his name.

He said, "Ray Brock."

Ray Brock? The foreign correspondent? International News Service? United Press? *The New York Times*? Profiler of dictators and diplomats in North Africa, Turkey, Pakistan, Israel, Iran, and elsewhere? Author of the best-seller *Blood, Oil and Sand*, which the review in *Commentary* said was full of "the globe-trotting journalist's standard mixture of frenetic prose, pointless anecdote, name-dropping, innuendo, aimless detail . . ."? Who was impersonating whom?

I had never heard of Ray Brock. I would look all that up later. But no one named Ray Brock could be the author of the book in my travel bag and also the alter ego of the protagonist preparing to fish a Navarrese river:

> Digging at the edge of the damp ground, I filled two empty
> tobacco-tins with worms and sifted dirt onto them. The goats
> watched me dig.

And then Jake Barnes and Bill Gorton start off on foot from a country inn. As they walk across a meadow and through rising woods and across high open fields and down to a stream, each successive sentence, in stairstep form, contains something of its predecessor and something new—repeating, advancing, repeating, advancing, like fracture zones on the bed of the ocean. It is not unaffective. It is lyrical. In future years, I would assign the passage to writing students, asking if they could see a way to shorten it without damaging the repetition.

Ray Brock died of a heart attack in 1968 in Orangeburg, New York. That he and Hemingway knew each other is indisputable. In a Hemingway collection in the Kennedy Library, in Boston, for example, are three letters from Brock to Hemingway with notations on them in Hemingway's handwriting. Brock was only fifty-four when he died. So, if he was the white-bearded papa at the table in Pamplona, he was forty at the time. His *Blood, Oil and Sand* had been published two years before. In a photograph on its dust jacket, he is interviewing a Turkish minister and the American Ambassador in Ankara. His beard is blacker than a diplomat's shoe.

Writer

Routinely, in winter months, Peter Benchley would pick me up in his car to go to an indoor court and play tennis with two others. Peter wrote at home. He lived on Boudinot Street, on the west side of the town of Princeton, where a great white shark was painted on the bottom of his swimming pool. He hadn't lived or written there long. In 1970, living in Pennington, eight miles from Princeton, he rented space in the back of a furnace factory with the purpose of writing a novel. He was nine years out of Harvard and had worked in television, written a travel book, and been a speechwriter for President Johnson. The novel, of course, was *Jaws*, published in 1974, and before long the Benchleys moved to Princeton. I worked then in rented space on Nassau Street across from the Princeton campus, and in the early winter of 1977 things were not going well. Nothing goes well in a piece of writing until it is in its final stages or done. One day, as usual, I couldn't wait for Peter to show up, and when he did I ran downstairs and across the street as if I were escaping. I jumped into his car, shouting, "Writing sucks. It sucks, stinks, and pukes. Writing sucks!" Peter turned at the corner and drove on wordlessly.

A few weeks later—same time, same curb—I got into Peter's car, and after turning the corner he said, "Remember that time you got into the car saying 'Writing sucks'?"

"How could I forget it?"

"If you made so much money that you would never have to write again, would you?"

I said, "Peter, that is your problem. That is so far off the scale in my case that I can't even think of an answer to the question."

I happened to know that Peter had netted eight million dollars in one recent year. (Eight million dollars then translates to thirty-eight million at this writing.) He could float forever on his raft above the shark in his pool.

But he did not. As things turned out for him, he had twenty-nine more years to live. Already, he had defeated some of the devils that defeat writing. In a friend's pool, before he had his own, he swam long distances almost every afternoon at cocktail time. Decades later, when pulmonary fibrosis overtook him in his sixties, he wrote his way past it as long as he could. Meanwhile, through the nineteen-eighties and nineteen-nineties, he never stopped writing, never stopped travelling to inform his writing— articles, screenplays, factual and fictional books. Out of his pool and into the Pacific Ocean, he swam into cages surrounded by real great whites, the better to tell about them. He found cinematic fiction in the Sea of Cortez. At home in Princeton, he ate lunch at a place called The Alchemist and Barrister, always at the same table, and with me frequently enough that I knew what he was writing and ceaselessly marvelled at the answer he was giving to the question he had asked me that time in his car in the early winter of 1977.

Beelining

The longest beeline distance in the forty-eight contiguous United States runs from Bellingham, Washington, to Boca Raton, Florida, two thousand seven hundred miles and change. Make the trip, I told myself—overland, on the surface, as close as possible to the beeline. Interview people as you encounter them. Like John Steinbeck. *Travels with Angus*. Like William Least Heat-Moon. *Brown highways*. Be coolly creative. Go from west to east.

There were alternatives. San Diego to Brewster, Massachusetts, twenty-six hundred and twenty-nine miles. Cape Mendocino to Cape Hatteras, twenty-four hundred and eighty-eight miles. But, length aside, Bellingham to Boca Raton would have been my choice. The beeline passes through eleven states in a sequence to some extent surprising: Washington, Idaho, Montana, Wyoming, Nebraska, Kansas, Missouri, Arkansas, Mississippi, Alabama, and Florida.

On a smaller scale, I did something like it with my two younger daughters when they were ten and seven, and in that experience this transcontinental ambition was rooted. We went from my brother's house, in Maryland, to my sister's house, in Ohio—three hundred and thirty miles as the bee flies. With a yardstick on a map, we drew a dark-pencil line and took off, staying about as close to that line as roads of any ilk and topography would allow. Right from the get-go, this trip beat the hell out of the interstate-highway system. In almost no time, we had crossed the Potomac River above Leesburg, Virginia, and passed close to Harpers Ferry and through the battlefield at Antietam. What young children would not sit up with educational interest in a scene where more than twenty thousand people fell in one day?

Seriatim, the beeline went through Maryland, then Virginia, then West Virginia, then Maryland, then Pennsylvania, and into Ohio. Maryland is one of the most misshapen states in the union, much more so than Vermont and New Hampshire, two goat legs reversed for packaging, and is right up there with bovine New York, its udder pendant, and with Louisiana, squatting, peeing into the Gulf. Along the straight southern border of Pennsylvania (the Mason-Dixon Line), Maryland extends westward an uncannily long thin arm, at one point so narrow that it separates Pennsylvania from West Virginia by 1.8 miles. Our beeline made the jump about there.

Pocahontas, Pennsylvania, 15552. Not much Pittsburgh envy

there, in those serene linear valleys of the deformed Appalachians. Off to our right a few miles was the field where United 93 would crash, twenty-eight years in the future. In Somerset, we came upon the Pennsylvania Turnpike dipping south and not far from the state line. Its vector westward, for the next forty miles, was right on our beeline. Where the turnpike bent away more pronouncedly northwest, we got off, and followed our line to McKeesport, Duquesne, Pittsburgh.

The principal oddity in this adventure was that a straight line between my brother's house in Maryland and my sister's house in Ohio went across Point State Park, the epicenter of Pittsburgh, where the Allegheny and Monongahela Rivers meet to form the Ohio River. Arriving from the southeast, we first crossed the mouth of the Monongahela, then stopped in Point Park to absorb the scene. Across the mouth of the Allegheny, on what Pittsburghers call the North Shore, was Three Rivers Stadium, home of the Pittsburgh Pirates, home of the Pittsburgh Steelers. Multipurpose stadiums were hot at the time and this one was three years old. It has since been replaced by a parking lot and scattered pop-up buildings, but in 1973, with its aerial city around it, it was in its immensity one of the seven wonders of Pennsylvania. Moreover, less than three months earlier—on December 23, 1972— the stadium had been the scene of the Immaculate Reception.

AFC divisional playoff, Raiders 7, Steelers 6, twenty-two seconds to go, no time-outs. Fourth and ten, Steelers on their own forty. Terry Bradshaw, pressured, throws a wild pass toward Frenchy Fuqua, twenty-five yards downfield. Raider Jack Tatum collides with Frenchy just as the ball arrives. End over end, it bounces backward off the Tatum-Fuqua collision and is received—plucked out of the air—by Pittsburgh's running back

Franco Harris, who is quickly in the Raiders' endzone and the Steelers win the game.

An implausible rule, rescinded six years later, said, in effect, that if the ball had touched Frenchy Fuqua, he was the only Pittsburgh player eligible to go on and catch it. Oakland thought so, thought the catch was maculate. Pittsburgh of course disagreed. The game's officials could not agree among themselves. Franco's catch will apparently stand forever as the Immaculate Reception. Of such materials are great legends made. In Pittsburgh.

Sewickley, Aliquippa, we continued north-northwest down the Ohio River—a counterintuitive fact if ever there was one—and after passing the mouth of the Beaver River crossed country to the state line. In Ohio, the most enduring memory from those last fifty miles began to develop when we went into a Kmart for something Martha wanted. Whatever it was, she knew exactly what it was and that Kmart carried it. A clerk was not helpful. A second clerk was not helpful. Martha said—not for the first time or the last—"I want to see the manager." She said it again until the manager came forth, and after a few minutes with him she was able to accomplish what she had come to accomplish. She was seven years old.

Like Jenny, Martha is a novelist now, but to help meet her family's expenses she long ago went frankly for money by writing pieces of nonfiction. She referred to this as "slumming."

One such piece was a form of beelining possible in only one place in the United States. The idea she sold was for a journey south to north on the San Andreas Fault. She invited me to come along as an unpaid guide. The driver was her husband, the poet Mark Svenvold. Roads are on the fault trace most of the way—on the Carrizo Plain, as in the Central Creeping Zone, and along

the shore of Bodega Bay. The San Andreas Fault, vastly superior
to Interstate 5, is in many ways the most attractive beeline in
California.

Walking the Province Line

In northwestern Princeton, a couple of hundred yards beyond
my house, is Province Line Road. If you look at modern maps
of New Jersey, on which this seventeenth-century province line
is not depicted, you can nonetheless discern it in the boundaries
of numerous townships, the boundaries of half a dozen counties,
and the scattered presence of local thoroughfares called Province
Line Road. South-southeast to north-northwest, these fragments
are cumulatively as straight as an arrow. After the Restoration and
the taking over of New Amsterdam by James, Duke of York, James
deeded New Jersey to Lord Berkeley and George Carteret. In the
sixteen-seventies, Lord Berkeley sold his half interest to Quakers.
The deed line dividing Carteret's East Jersey from the Quakers'
West Jersey was not surveyed until 1687. Stone pylons from that
survey still dot the province line. Settled by a few farmers, the town
of Princeton was four years old when the pylons came.

If I go out of my house to Province Line Road and turn left, I
go downhill past a house that the novelist John O'Hara built and
named Linebrook, and continue a short way to Stony Brook, on the
far side of which is the Educational Testing Service, home of the
S.A.T. I'm doing that on foot and never in a car, because Princeton's Province Line Road, one of the oldest roads in the state, has
a gap there, has never made it past a diabase outcrop that forms a

puny cliff negotiable by horse and buggy but not by automobile. One of my parents' friends tried to go down that way in his Lincoln Continental Cabriolet, which later required a winch to be recovered. An old quarterback, he was fond of Old Crow. The province-line bridge over Stony Brook rusted and rotted to an extent that caused it to be closed in 1981. After thirty years, it was rescued sufficiently to become a footbridge, which it is today, closed to automobiles. So the Province Line Road in Princeton alone is perforated by two hiatuses and if you want to take it in you are best off walking.

My English friend H. G. T. P. Doyne-Ditmas, of MI5, loved the province line as he loved antiques in general. We had known each other and been in varied academic settings together since we were teen-aged. As a professional spook, he came from London with some frequency to Langley, Virginia, and he usually stopped off to see us in Princeton, sometimes to urge me out the door to walk the province line. When we turned north, we went down into the Hopewell Valley, and across it, passing rural homes, developed farmland, The Solid Rock ("First Born Church of the Living God"), and a stone monument that bears in bronze a map of the province line. Then came the flat-topped Sourland Mountain. Addressing it, the asphalt way jumps a few hundred yards west to skirt long-private property and its name soon changes to Lindbergh Road. Charles Lindbergh built a substantial house on this road four years after his flight to Paris. He moved to the elongate flat-topped mountain because he envisioned a major airport there, with planes landing on the high surface, free for tens of miles from concern about higher surroundings. The Lindberghs called their house Highfields. Charles Augustus Lindbergh Jr., born in 1930, was kidnapped from Highfields twenty months later. Anybody who goes there unauthorized today had better be prepared to get out fast, even if he can claim to be James Bond. Signs on Lindbergh Road, beside the mouth of the long driveway, mention the New Jersey Juvenile Justice Commission. Highfields is part of New Jersey's prison system.

On the far side of the mountain, we rejoined the province line, the Hunterdon-Somerset county line, here called Rainbow Hill Road. It rose steeply, then plunged to a rushing stream, then ascended gradually through farmland to Clover Hill. Understand, in this part of New Jersey, words like "mountain," "mount," and even "hill" are hardworking euphemisms. These topographic lumps are not what they were named to be. Central New Jersey was part of a large Jurassic lake that ran about a hundred miles from Newark to Reading, Pennsylvania, and was the result of a stretching of the crust of the earth that tore open relatively small basins like this one and the very large basin of the Atlantic Ocean, which is still widening, nearly two and a half inches a year. That is tectonism on an operatic scale, and this so-called Newark Basin is not. But the lake lasted a most unusual eight million years, and collected a lot of sediment, which turned into rock, and lava flows, which solidified. For a hundred and fifty million years, those sedimentary and igneous laminations have eroded differentially, exposing the harder rock that we call hills and mountains. Clover Hill. The province line measures the width of the Newark Basin, twenty-one miles shore to shore, Princeton to Annandale. Clover Hill is exactly halfway across the Jurassic lake.

This was antique enough for Doyne-Ditmas and he loved Clover Hill. A Reformed church and its graveyard are dominant there, not a difficult place to dominate, just a rural crossroads.

He savored the surnames in the graveyard—Pipho, Polhemus, Schlapfer, Schwake—as anyone called Doyne-Ditmas might be wont to do, but what attracted him most were the people born at the end of the eighteenth century, the people for whom the bell in Philadelphia cracked, the would-have-been Brits who got away. For example, Jacob Nevius 1769–1857, Hannah Lanning Nevius 1792–1857, Sarah Schanck 1792–1831, Paul Kuhl Dilts 1785–1881, Sarah Sharp Dilts 1793–1877. Among the dead in that graveyard, one of five was a Nevius, a Polhemus, or a Dilts. Twenty-seven were surnamed Dilts, and others bore the name folded in, like Sarah Dilts Kinney and Sarah Dilts Hoagland. Abraham Van Arsdale Polhemus 1800–1843 was there with his family under two or three tons of granite. A large and beautiful red oak shaded other graves nearby. Theodore P. Dilts was twenty-four years old when he died in 1928. Dory Dilts Road is three miles away, on the province line.

The church was built in 1834. Wood frame. Fish-scale clapboard around the front entrance. Lancet windows down the sides, two stories tall. Cupola. Belfry. Gothic Revival spirelets at the high front corners. The church and its surroundings are in the National Register of Historic Places. Peter G. Dilts, the graveyard's senior tenant, was born in 1717 and died in 1801, Sarah Schanck died in 1831. Either they were disinterred somewhere and moved, or they were waiting in the ground when the church arrived, Doyne-Ditmas cannily observed. Supporting his analysis, he pointed out that there were two sandstone slabs commemorating the same Peter G. Dilts 1717–1801. The more weathered stone was leaning against the later one, which was firm and plumb. It suggested that in 1834 Peter G. Dilts and his 1801 gravestone were transplanted.

On my own, I would not have lingered in that cemetery a tenth as long as Doyne-Ditmas did, so I can easily say that I owe all these facts to the mind of an undercover agent.

That was as far as we got, Hal and I, walking the province line. He drifted out of the MI5 and into the Department of Transport, where he was in charge of security for everything that rolled, flew, or floated in the U.K. He supervised all security involved in the construction of the Chunnel. My work took me to Britain now and again, and he helped me with projects there. We planned a return to Clover Hill and a walk up the line to Annandale, but Hal developed cancer and died. He lies in the cemetery of a church called St. Swithin's in the Meadow. Harold Granville Terence Payne Doyne-Ditmas 1930–2016.

From Clover Hill to Dory Dilts Road to Annandale is about thirteen miles. At Annandale, the province line crosses I-78, whose east-west route exactly sketches the maximum local advance of the continental ice of the Pleistocene. Native Americans immemorially travelled along the ice sheet's terminal moraine, making with their feet the trail that has become the interstate highway. Lakes to the north are where ice gouged deepest into stream valleys. Lakes to the south are where people have dammed rivers. To the south are plenty of clues that ice in great thickness was somewhere nearby— periglacial boulders, pitted outwash plains, gravels flushed forth and piled up in such quantity that euphemistic New Jersey would call it Mt. Holly. On the south side of I-78, New Jersey landscape is Delaware's, on the north side Vermont's. New Jersey's northwestern counties do resemble Vermont, and for the same glacial reason. Eight hundred young people in Annandale did not come for the scenery. They are inmates at the Mountainview Youth Correctional

Facility, one more prison on the province line. Assaults have been common there. Inmates have murdered inmates: Carl J. Epps Jr. 1990–2010, Joshua Jones 1989–2012.

The province line is a hundred and seven miles long. Doyne-Ditmas and I covered nine. If we could have stayed at it, we would still be out there grave watching, trespassing, ascending the deformed Appalachians, listening to Pine Barrens tree frogs. Twenty-five miles south of Princeton, the province line bisects the military reservation known as Fort Dix. In the western part is McGuire Air Force Base, where cargo planes are so large that the Wright brothers' entire first flight would fit inside one. East of the line is Naval Air Engineering Station Lakehurst, where Deutsche Zeppelin-Reederei's hydrogen-borne LZ-129, the Hindenburg, coming to its mooring mast after a trip from Frankfurt, exploded in flame in 1937, killing only sixteen of the ninety-seven people aboard but nonetheless ending, apparently forever, the era of the big rigid airships. Inside Lakehurst's Hangar No. 1—a thousand feet long, two hundred feet high, and the Hindenburg's New Jersey home—pigeons became the predominant aircraft.

Arneytown, four miles up the line from Fort Dix, has its own Province Line Road and, beside it, the Brigadier General William C. Doyle Memorial Cemetery, designed for a hundred and seventy-one thousand veterans and their families, under ground-level stones. In the Pine Barrens once, farther south, I heard General Doyle deliver a eulogy at a small and isolated clearing in the forest beside a monument bearing the Aztec Eagle. This was where the pilot Emilio Carranza, "Mexico's Lindbergh," son of the president of Mexico, crashed and died in 1928 on an intended nonstop flight from New York to Mexico City. On July 12, 1966, anniversary of the day Carranza died, Mexicans from New York, New Jersey, and as far away as Chicago, many in brightly colored Mexican dress, were there, as annually, to make speeches and music. They did not really need General Doyle to be there to say: "Here in New Jersey's pine country, the gallant airman was grounded forever. He was not dess-tined to complete his mission."

The northern terminus of the line is on the Delaware River close to and about twelve hundred vertical feet below Sunfish Pond on the Appalachian Trail. This terrain, God knows, is not the Rocky Mountain front, but neither is it Mt. Holly or an erosional hump in the Newark Basin. Sunfish Pond and the Appalachian Trail are on Kittatinny Ridge in the deformed Appalachians. Called by various names in its extraordinary length, the ridge runs from Alabama to Newfoundland and you can even find it in France and Sweden. It is a result of the intercontinental collisions that assembled Pangaea four-hundred-and-some-odd million years ago. As landmasses came together, they folded the crust in the way that a bent fender will crinkle or a cloth will fold if pushed from opposite sides of a table. At this latitude, such folded and faulted ridges, in parallel sinuosity, run all the way across Pennsylvania to the Allegheny Plateau, not far from Pittsburgh. This big ridge in New Jersey, though, is locally on its own, because across the river in Pennsylvania are the so-called Poconos, fake mountains that might as well be in the Newark Basin near Princeton, erosional remnants, nothing more, in a small plateau (the Pocono Plateau) that took the shock of the tectonics and did not buckle. Sunfish Pond, forty-four acres, is natural, glacial, beautiful in its setting. Its setting was long ago noticed for other reasons. If Sunfish Pond were enlarged in depth, width, and length, it could hold even more water, and the water could be pumped up there out of the Delaware River, stored in the magnified pond, then—in hours of peak need—let out to fall through hydroelectric turbines and be on its way downriver. At this writing, the project is still just a thought.

Colonial Americans consistently referred to the land between the Hudson and the Delaware as "the Jerseys." Disputes in the sixteen-eighties, sixteen-nineties, and as late as 1743 produced new versions of the dividing line, all rooted, as the original one is, in Little Egg Harbor, near the sand that has become Atlantic City. Collectively, the varying province lines go north closely, like a tall shoot of prairie grass, splaying, but not widely, at the blades. The first line, the one that comes up like pentimento as intrastate boundaries on modern road maps, the one with the pylons in it, the one that goes past my house, is the one I mean when I say province line.

The first European living at Little Egg Harbor was Falkenberg the linguist. He moved there in the sixteen-nineties from an island in the Delaware River, a part of New Sweden. He already owned eight hundred acres of the coastal land, having bought it many years earlier from the Lenni Lenape, the New Jersey tribe that now lives in Oklahoma as "Delawares." Falkenberg spoke their language, served as an interpreter. He brokered land sales by Lenape to Quakers.

Between Little Egg Harbor and Fort Dix lies the twenty-five per cent of New Jersey known since colonial times as the Pine Barrens. I would love to have hiked with Doyne-Ditmas there, where I had hiked a great deal before. The province line goes through what are known as the dwarf forests, the pygmy forests—about

twelve thousand acres where you can see over the tops of mature
oaks and mature pitch pines, stunted by centuries of frequent fire.
Ocean County on one side, Burlington County on the other, it
passes through Brendan T. Byrne State Forest, where the same species are seventy feet tall, as they are generally in the Pine Barrens,
which were state and federally preserved, under Byrne's impetus
and leadership, when he was Governor of New Jersey.

Whitesbog is in Byrne State Forest, where Joseph White, in
the earliest days of the twentieth century, was the foremost producer of cranberries in the pinelands. One of his four daughters
was Elizabeth, who, in her twenties, read a theoretical article by
Frederick Coville, of the federal Department of Agriculture, about
the possibility of crossbreeding wild-blueberry bushes to evolve a
larger berry. The Pine Barrens are almost universally underbrushed
with wild blueberries. She wrote to Coville and invited him to
come to the farm and undertake the project with her, which he
did. She gave small boards with various-sized holes in them to
all local people who were interested, and said that she would pay
for blueberry bushes at a rate scaled to the size of the largest hole
that the berries would not go through. Soon, she and Coville had
a hundred and twenty bushes. They chose two, and, from them,
made thirty-five thousand hybrid cuttings, which they grew into
bushes, among which they chose four, from which modern cul-
tivated blueberries, in their numerous varieties, were developed.

Elizabeth White's first commercial shipment was in 1916. In
1952, when the Garden State Parkway was under construction,
she invited landscape architects from the state highway department to Whitesbog and showed them through her blueberry
fields. As I described this scene long ago,

Miss White was over six feet tall, she carried a cane and wore a Whistler's Mother dress that was as neat as a pin. Her ankles were black from the dirt of the fields, and her hands were midnight-blue from the wax of the berries. In her home she served each of her visitors a blueberry that was the size of a baseball, as they recall it, heaped over with sugar and resting in a pool of cream. Then she asked them to consider planting blueberry bushes along the Garden State Parkway. Miss White died a few months after that. Blueberry bushes were planted later in profusion on the margins of the parkway where it runs along the edge of the Pine Barrens.

Clarksville, on the province line, is less than two miles south of Princeton. Described on the Internet as "an unincorporated community in Lawrence Township," it is where the line crosses route U.S. 1. When I was a student at Princeton High School, in the nineteen-forties, I had four friends whose families were significant parts of that unincorporated community. Bob Dilatush and Dolores Dilatush, brother and sister, grew up on a farm that filled the northeast corner of the intersection. Bea Coleman and Lew Coleman, cousins, grew up on a pair of farms in the southeast corner of the intersection. Seven or eight years later, my friend Tom Godolphin and his wife were renting a farmhouse in the northwest quadrant of the intersection. Around there today, it is much easier to drive than to walk the province line. The Dilatush farm became American Cyanamid. The Coleman farms became Quaker Bridge Mall. Godolphin's farm became the fifty-nine stores of Nassau Park Pavilion—Dick's Sporting Goods, Home Depot, Walmart, Target, Best Buy, Wegmans, Chuck E. Cheese . . .

It was near the north end of the province line that Winona of the Lenape leaped to her death from a cliff of what her people called the Endless Mountain. Part folklore, part legend, it is a seventeenth-century story in which a Dutch miner, there to work the ridge for copper, goes out hunting by the river and aims his rifle at a chattering squirrel. He shoots, misses. He aims again, shoots, misses. Getting his act together, he aims once more, fires, and the squirrel falls to the ground. He picks it up. Its body has been pierced by an arrow. He looks around. By the edge of the river, Winona throws him a smile from her red canoe. They fall in love. Over time, she tells him the history of the river and the Endless Mountain. New Amsterdam shuts down and he is ordered home. It is not in him to take an Indian wife to Europe. He tells her so on that cliff above the river. She jumps to her death and he follows.

Jenny Jump Mountain is twelve miles from that scene, south on the province line, and in those twelve miles the line crosses the Great Valley of the Appalachians—twenty-five hundred miles long, and elsewhere called Shenandoah, Hudson, Champlain, Tennessee, Clinch River Valley. The crystalline rock of Jenny Jump Mountain is nearly a billion years older than the deformed Appalachians, and is of a continuous piece with the Green Mountains, the Berkshires, the Great Smoky Mountains. On either side of the valley, something about the mountains at this latitude, bisected by the province line, has given rise to lugubrious legends. This one is inverse to Winona's: Jenny, of no known surname, was collecting berries at a cliff edge on the mountain when she was menaced, or thought she was, by a Lenape brave. Her father called to her and told her to jump. Presumably, he was going to catch her. He didn't, and she died. Her spirit has been seen by local people many times. This is the point on the province line most closely associated with Halloween. Ghost Lake is there, and Shades of Death Road.

Fossils were discovered on the province line in 1980—thirteen miles south of Princeton, in Ellisdale, New Jersey, on Ellisdale's Province Line Road. Twenty thousand specimens have since been removed, all to the New Jersey State Museum, other collectors prohibited. This is on the modern coastal plain and is in no way related to the Newark Basin and the Jurassic lake—curious withal that three species of dinosaur have been found there. Also, three kinds of amphibian. Salamanders. Possums. Cimolodons. Crocodilians. Turtles. Lizards. Myriad bony fishes. Rays.

The geology describes a brackish marsh behind a barrier beach at the mouth of a stream, radiometrically dated as seventy-six to eighty million years before the present, in the Campanian Age of Upper Cretaceous time. Every skeleton has been disarticulated—that is, whole skeletons have not been found there. Instead, the trove is a condensed boneyard of terrestrial species, marine species, and river species, washed together, the geology reveals, by the high and surging waters of a single storm.

The Safe Houses of Suburbia

Before touching this topic, if I had a ten-foot pole I would look around for a longer one. As I ride my bicycle among the elegant streets in my suburban town, I've been wondering, for a decade or two, about certain houses I go by. There is no evidence of families in them. They seem in other ways anomalous. They bring out the investigative reporter in me. What goes on in these places? Or doesn't go on? I ride on. The investigative reporter in me has never been ambitious.

Let me offer three examples before I retreat into my own house and lock the door.

1. A sprawling ranch on several acres has a short asphalt driveway that pools into a parking area that can accommodate five cars. There is no garage. In my own car, I often drive by there at night, and have never seen a light. Not only is the house dark and lifeless, but also there are no cars. These people can't be vacationing in Nantucket, methinks, unless they are up there in winter as well as summer. Every other week, yellow plastic barrels line the street, but this place never recycles. Yet cars collect there mornings soon after nine. Three cars, sometimes five. You don't have to work for *The Washington Post* to imagine that people are working in this house. At what? The nearest office park is five miles away. This place, with its daytime cars, its absence of any sign of family life, its all-around anonymity, is also secluded. Secluding what? How many people show up in the cars? Are they wearing ties?

2. A sprawling ranch on several acres, market value in seven digits, has been evidently unoccupied for fifteen years, but no realty sign has gone up there, let alone a notice of a tax deed sale. Somebody is keeping the place up, and something is keeping the place closed. Why? Wherefore? There's a car in the front yard, off the driveway, near the road, which probably suggests life and occupancy to most people driving by. From a bicycle, though, you are more than aware that this vehicle's four tires are flat, and that

weeds are growing out through the apertures in the hubcaps. This is a scene in search of a story. If I were writing it, I would go up to the house, peer in the windows, and count the skeletons.

3. On a corner lot off the southern slope of the Princeton Ridge, a two-story house went up twenty years ago, architecturally a large and simple box with a gable roof and no distinguishing features—or, perhaps closer to purpose, a distinguishing absence of features. I mean, the house has been there twenty years and has no curtains in its windows. It has a lawn, yes, but no additional landscaping, not so much as a bush, let alone a tree. Garage doors are shut. For all the use they get, they could be painted on a wall. The place is so naked it resembles the model houses developers put up before they build two hundred like them. There is no sign of children. No sign of adult occupants. Who is doing what at that house? "Living there" is the first thought to vanish. Is it some kind of exchange, known only as such to people who drop in for minutes at a time, something changing hands here who knows when? This is New Jersey, Jimmy. Would it work best as a one-off or a series? In any case, you do it. Better you. I still have miles to go on my ride.

Joseph Henry House

I teach in a house on the Princeton campus that has been, to say the least, peripatetic. When I was in grade school half a block away, it was on the corner of Nassau Street and Washington Road, and was the residence of a dean named Christian Gauss. That was its third location. It had been designed by the physicist Joseph Henry, a pioneer in electromagnetism, and built in 1838 as his home. His not-exactly-portable home. Two and a half stories. Brick. A five-bay façade. By 1946, when I was in Princeton High School, the house had worn out its welcome at the Gauss location, because it crowded the footprint of a new university library that would contain seventy miles of shelves. With an engineering rationale totally lost on the likes of me, the library excavation was largely accomplished before the house was moved. The excavation was surely the largest hole in the ground that Princeton has ever seen. Iceberg fashion, most of the new library would be below grade—three vast floors filling the excavated acreage. East to west, the house was moved along the edge of the chasm. It may not have teetered but seemed to. It was finally settled on its present foundation, on the front campus, off one corner of Nassau Hall, the college's principal and oldest building. Joseph Henry House, as it is called, was soon occupied by still another dean.

This one's son was Tom Godolphin. We had been friends since the elementary years. At twelve or so, we had hit golf balls over the roof of the university's McCarter Theater, shelling the other side. We would be classmates in college. Soon thereafter, in the Godolphins' living room, which would one day be filled by a long table for seminars like mine, Tom Godolphin and Diana Ashforth were married, in front of the fireplace, while I sat on a couch opposite with Henrietta Oates.

The last dean—Aaron Lemonick—left the house in 2000, when the Council of the Humanities took it over, turning bedrooms into offices. Dean of the Faculty, he was a tough-minded physicist. Asked at a large meeting what the university's best strategy should be in building a first-rate faculty, he said, right back, "Hire compulsives and leave them alone."

But I have drifted forward more than half a century. In June, 1947, the event occurred that would cause me—about twenty years later—to plan to write a piece from these notes. In June, 1947, Princeton was celebrating its two-hundredth year in higher education. The fact that this milestone had come along in 1946 was not a discrepancy of sufficient magnitude to disturb anyone, including, certainly, a faculty whose concept of the best three months of the academic year was "June, July, and August." Actually, there was no discrepancy at all. Princeton ballyhooed its bicentennial year from September 1946 onward, building toward a grand finale on June 17, 1947, when I had just finished my junior year in high school, Tom his at Exeter.

We watched from his second-floor bedroom in Joseph Henry House. Below us were five thousand people, most of them on folding chairs arranged, with aisles, across the front lawn of Nassau Hall. In the eighteenth century, it had been the largest building in colonial America, and the Continental Congress met there for six or seven months during the American Revolution. Tom and I each sat in an open window, our legs dangling above the crowd. These seats were surely the most advantaged, the best in the house. The academic procession passed right below us and curled around the big lawn, its destination an elevated platform. There was Harry S. Truman, President of the United States. Sixteen years later, the President of the United States would be assassinated by a gunman standing at the open window of a warehouse for textbooks. Five years beyond that, Martin Luther King Jr. would be assassinated by a gunman in Memphis, and, two months after that, Robert Kennedy, in Los Angeles. But this Princeton event was forty-six years and two world wars after the most recent presidential assassination, which quite obviously was not uppermost in people's minds. In 1996—Princeton's semiquincentennial—President Clinton would show up in this same space and it would be completely surrounded by existing and ad hoc wrought-iron fencing, an immense cage with metal detectors at the few points of entry and the Secret Service everywhere.

Walking with Truman were Herbert Hoover, the thirty-first President of the United States, and General Dwight D. Eisenhower, the future thirty-fourth. There was Fleet Admiral Chester W. Nimitz, Commander in Chief, U.S. Pacific Fleet. Field Marshal Viscount Alexander of Tunis, Governor General of Canada. Fred M. Vinson, of Kentucky, once a Congressman, then Secretary of the Treasury, now Chief Justice of the U.S. Supreme Court—one of few people ever to serve in all three branches of the federal government. Alfred E. Driscoll, Governor of New Jersey. Judge Learned Hand, Second Circuit Court of Appeals. Albert Einstein, of the Institute for Advanced Study, five blocks from his home and, rumpled, appearing to have slept late. Eugène Cardinal Tisserant. Serge Koussevitzky. T. S. Eliot.

This procession was a thousand people long and was not done yet. From many other universities, teams of emissaries, whole cadres of delegates, had come to march, too, and they were lined up, more or less, in order of antiquity. The University of Toulouse (1229). Take that, Harvard! The University of Salamanca (1218). Take that, Yale! Cambridge (1209). The Sorbonne (1150). Oxford (1096).

Workouts with Princeton Coaches

As head coach of men's lacrosse at Princeton, Bill Tierney won six national championships, but that did nothing for his fly casting, at which he was, and seems to have remained, a novice. One autumn morning, we tried to address the problem by having a one-on-one fly-casting workout on the Astroturf of his lacrosse stadium. Trying for distance, trying for the drapefold rhythm of the cast, we were throwing flies that not only were barbless but had no hooks at all. I had snipped them off with wire cutters. No one else was in or around the stadium to observe this insane diorama and possibly call 911.

The air was cool, the sky was clear, and we had been casting for about half an hour when suddenly we were drenched with flying water. It seemed like an act of God. The fishermen go not to the waters; the waters go to the fishermen. What next? A smallmouth? A crappie? What we did next was retreat. Session over. Soaking wet. This was the lacrosse stadium, yes, but it was also the stadium of field hockey, a sport that calls for a damp surface to reduce friction.

I have spent a lifetime around Princeton coaches, my father having been their teams' physician. The head coach of football was our next-door neighbor while my age was pushing ten. Yesterday, I went eleven miles on bicycles with Mitch Henderson, the men's basketball coach. I'm writing this in 2020, aged eighty-nine. The bizarrerie of the Bill Tierney fly-casting scene caused me to plan a piece of writing about workouts with varied coaches in various sports over the years, but I never got around to it and will condense the concept here. When I was in my middle teens, I played chess now and again with the incumbent basketball coach. Cappy Cappon was his name and he didn't always win. In the same junior-high and high-school years, Coach Eddie Donovan taught me squash and golf almost from scratch, and added what he could to my tennis game. Eddie coached J.V. football, freshman basketball, and varsity baseball for whole annals of time, and the sort of patient generosity he showed this teen-ager was characteristic of him all the way. Pete Carril, who is only seven months older than I am, came to Princeton as head coach of basketball in 1967, and that was the beginning of more than half a century of workouts with him, in which I have learned and learned again that perseverance does not always pay off. In earlier years, we played lunchtime basketball in the gym, guarding each other, he with a cigar in his mouth. In winter, we played singles and doubles squash, and in summer tennis, he with a cigar in his mouth. If he took it out and left it smoldering under the net, I knew I was playing over my head. And that leaves us, for present purposes, with Dutch Schoch.

He came to Princeton in 1938, as an assistant crew coach, when he was twenty-four years old. When he was fifty-six, and standing over a birdie putt on the fourth green of Princeton's golf course, he died of a heart attack. Five years earlier, his heart condition had forced him to give up as head coach of the heavyweight crew, a job he had done with much success for twenty years. He had been on the golf team at the University of Washington, and Princeton moved him from lake to links as coach of golf. About then—in the middle nineteen-sixties—we began playing squash together, in winter, at least once a week.

Dutch was a big guy, robust, life-loving, ebullient, profane. His record included the time he was thrown off the Ohio River for profanity on his bullhorn. Yes, he had somehow played competitive golf at the University of Washington but he was primarily an oarsman and had been one of the celebrated "boys in the boat." He was rowing with them in Poughkeepsie in their first great national victory, head-to-head with Cornell. When he got his Olympic gold, in Germany in 1936, he was one of Washington's two alternates.

And now, across the late nineteen-sixties, he was playing squash with me, never showing the slightest discomfort with this spectacular devolution—no gloom, no disappointment, just his ever-forward-moving enthusiasm. Not for nothing is the trophy for the annual mano a mano in rowing between the University of Washington and the University of California named for him.

Eventually came the day toward which this recollection is pointed. In a tight, consuming match, we split the first two games, and thus a third and deciding game was meant to occur. Dutch's face, though, had reddened to an extraordinary extent. He was breathing heavily, and his head looked like a large tomato. Aware of his heart condition, I thought he might die right there. I felt sure he should not play the third game. What to do? Breathing heavily, I leaned back against a wall of the court and slid down it slowly until my butt hit the floor. I said, "Dutch, I can't do it. I can't go on. I have to quit now. I'm exhausted."

His deep voice booming, he said, "You little bastard, get up and serve."

I got up and served. After we finished, he went outside, got into his Jeep, and drove home.

The Commemorations of Woodrow Wilson

When Woodrow Wilson was coaching football at Wesleyan University, he lived in a frame house on the campus. This set of facts has not been prominent in Wilson's curriculum vitae, but is well known to Isobel McPhee, daughter of my daughter Laura. Isobel's room at Wilson House when she was a student at Wesleyan had been Woodrow Wilson's bedroom.

In 2020, the year in which I'm writing this, certain other facts from Wilson's life—obscure and obscured—have caused Princeton University to remove his name from its Woodrow Wilson School of Public and International Affairs and from one of its residential colleges. In a season of iconoclasm, he was the broad side of a barn, since his legacy included anti-Semitism and systemic racism. An 1879 Princeton graduate, Wilson earned his Ph.D. in history and political science at Johns Hopkins, taught a couple of years at Bryn Mawr and at Wesleyan, and in 1890 returned to Princeton, where he designed a widely copied pre-law curriculum and was voted year after year the college's most popular professor. He became its president in 1902. Originating academic departments, creating deanships, he literally turned Princeton into a university. He appointed the first Jew to the faculty. And he created the preceptorial system (small discussion classes with as few as five students and a professor), for which he doubled the size of the faculty. In the pressure of it all, he suffered a severe stroke in 1906.

In that year also, he got into heavy controversy with Andrew Fleming West, Dean of the Graduate School. In fact to this day it is known as the Wilson-West Controversy, and it split this town apart. The basic issue had to do with the construction of residential quarters for graduate students. Wilson wanted them to be central on the college campus. Contemptuous of the behavior of undergraduates, West wanted to build a graduate college the better part of a mile away. People took sides, thought became anger, and bitterness developed that went much deeper than the question that began it. When I was a child, thirty years later, there were Wilson-West veterans in Princeton who still crossed the street to avoid encountering one another on the sidewalk.

As an undergraduate in the nineteen-fifties, I was various forms of editor of three student magazines, and I undertook to acquaint my peers with the Wilson-West Controversy. I needed most of all a person who had been on campus at the time and who could give me in an interview an unbiased account of the fight. In Princeton, there was no one. At least it was obvious that none of the old-timers I talked to were qualified, and none of them was able to say who might be, until someone mentioned Sigmund Spaeth. Sigmund Spaeth? He was a musicologist, a show-business figure, "The Tune Detective," famous on the radio, scarcely at Princeton. His brother, though, was the Shakespearean scholar John Duncan Spaeth, long a star of the Princeton faculty, and—in the Wilson-West era—Sigmund had been an instructor in the English Department while earning his Ph.D. at Princeton with his thesis "Milton's Knowledge of Music."

I wrote to Sigmund Spaeth, asking for an interview, and his reply said that would be fine but I would have to come to a New York hospital because that is where he was. I went to the city and the hospital room, where I found him looking like a *New Yorker* cartoon. One leg was in a cast from ankle to hip and held in the air at a forty-five-degree angle by a rope-and-pulley fixed to the ceiling. I told him that I had been told in Princeton that he was maybe the only person in the world who could give me a clear, unbiased account of the Wilson-West Controversy.

He said that was correct, cleared his throat, and began with these exact words: "That son of a bitch West . . ."

In 1910, a benefactor left in his will enough money backing West to cause Wilson to say to his wife, "We've beaten the living but we can't fight the dead."

Wilson resigned and went into politics, which, otherwise, he might never have done. He was elected Governor of New Jersey in that same year, 1910, and two years later, President of the United States. During the next forty years, in the undying embers of Wilson-West, no statue, monument, building, icon, or other form of outdoor proclamation on the Princeton campus commemorated the fact that this thirteenth president of the university had been the twenty-eighth President of the United States. He was as absent from honor in 1920, '30, '40, '50 as he would again become in 2020. In an archway that runs through 1879 Hall, which was a gift to the college from Wilson's class at its tenth reunion, is a bronze plaque that lists all the names of the students of '79, "Thomas Woodrow Wilson" one from the bottom. That plaque today is again the only sign of him on the campus.

Back up the Riverbank

In the rapids just below our fishing cabin on the upper Delaware River, and no more than a couple of hundred yards upstream and downstream, I have caught American eels, American shad, rainbow trout, brown trout, lampreys, smallmouth bass, rock bass, sunfish, fallfish, yellow perch, crappies, catfish, hickory shad, suckers, and walleyes. I have not caught the white perch, gizzard shad, largemouth bass, and striped bass, but not for lack of trying. The message of this list of nineteen species is not entirely "Bug off, this is my querencia," but is also a reference to a catalogue of writing subjects that I once meant to undertake but chose instead a fisherman's strategic silence—in every instance but one. American shad were the subject of my book *The Founding Fish*, large parts of which were written in the cabin. But I am walking up the riverbank now, and with no further intention than to eat what is in my creel.

World Premiere

Tom Vennum was an ethnomusicologist at the Smithsonian Institution. Born in Minnesota, he retired to Madeline Island, Wisconsin, in Lake Superior, where he had spent almost every summer of his life. The Ojibwe tribe was all around him there, and the title of one of his books is *The Ojibwa Dance Drum*. The drummer Mickey Hart, of the Grateful Dead, read *The Ojibwa Dance Drum* and before long Tom Vennum was onstage with the Dead, being introduced to successive crowds.

Tom wrote a book on the Ojibwe gathering of wild rice. He wrote a book called *American Indian Lacrosse: Little Brother of War*. Political disagreements were settled on lacrosse fields, winner take all. From Cherokee shootouts to the trick-play capture of Fort Michilimackinac, in 1763, the stories are off the charts and into the Hollywood zone. Tom was close to the family of a student of mine named Pete Bell, who twice arranged for Tom to come to the class and be interviewed and profiled. Tom asked a favor. He was completing a documentary film on the skills and methods of Earl Nyholm, an Ojibwe who made bark canoes in the ancient way. A foundation was paying for it in three contractual stages. The final payment would not be forthcoming until the finished film had been introduced at a university. Could I make that happen?

I could try. I asked the Dean of the Faculty, who suggested that I ask the Dean of the College, who suggested that I "run it by" the Provost, who suggested that I mention it to the Dean of the Faculty. I tried the chairs of Anthropology, History, Art History, English, and Civil Engineering. And at last I thought of Alfred Bush, a librarian, Curator of Western Americana in the Harvey S. Firestone Memorial Library. Alfred was an old friend and I vented my frustration. He said, "John, you are going about this in the wrong way. If you want to get something done around here, go to the undergraduates. Go to the Native American undergraduates. They have a sort of club."

A day would come when a student in my course would write a piece about a pow-wow she went to in Philadelphia with her classmate Emery Real Bird, president of Natives at Princeton, but this was sixteen years before that and I had no awareness of Native American undergraduates at Princeton, let alone that they were organized. But I quickly found Micah Treuer, their president (who, incidentally, happened to be an Ojibwe), and he quickly proved Alfred Bush right.

Micah arranged a presentation of the bark-canoe film in McCosh 50, a four-hundred-and-sixty-five-seat lecture hall with a projection booth and a screen big enough for a bark canoe at twelve inches to the foot. When the day arrived, the film's premiere audience consisted of Tom Vennum, me, and a handful of students, half of them Indians.

The Leghorn Syndrome

Trajan. The name is enough to give you pallesthesia. The Emperor Trajan (53–117 C.E.). Diadumenian, Vespasian, Domitian, Diocletian—these names alone are enough to conquer the world one syllable at a time. Hadrian. Hostilian. Aurelian. Valerian. Write makes might. Aemilian. Valentinian. Majorian. Justinian. Where did the Romans get these tolling and reverberating, thrilling appellations?

They didn't. The names are English for the likes of Traianus, Vespasianus, Domitianus, and Diocletianus. You can't blame the English. In Surrey, that suffix just won't do. Yet there's more to this than that. Once, in a train station in Basel—multilingual Basel—I heard a testy British voice under a bowler hat say, "Why con't someone hyuh speak a decent language?" The English are not characteristically attracted to Continental speech. They call Livorno Leghorn. They are rife with Leghorn syndrome. Symptomatic are Rome, Naples, Milan, Venice, and Florence, less so the Forum and the Colosseum. The Emperor Volition, Mindful of Nutrition . . .

Burlesquoni take it from here.

North East Rising Sun

I can wax polemical about titles. Editors—as a general class from print to the Internet—seem to think titles are like chicken heads. They can cut them off without additional effect on the C.V. of the chicken. They can replace each one with their own idea of the head of an improved chicken.

This is not my first fulmination on the topic. In *Draft No. 4*, a 2017 book on the writing process, I said that a title "should be a flashlight that shines down into the story," and testily went on to develop the point as follows:

> Editors of every ilk seem to think that titles are their prerogative—that they can buy a piece, cut the title off the top, and lay on one of their own. When I was young, this turned my skin pink and caused horripilation. I should add that I encountered such editors almost wholly at maga-

zines other than *The New Yorker*—*Vogue, Holiday, The Sat-urday Evening Post*. The title is an integral part of a piece of writing, and one of the most important parts, and ought not to be written by anyone but the writer of what follows the title. Editors' habit of replacing an author's title with one of their own is like a photo of a tourist's head on the cardboard body of Mao Zedong.

In 1955, in the train room of New York's Pennsylvania Station, I listened to the sonorous, almost echoing announcements not only of departing westbound trains but also of trains on the Long Island Rail Road. One of those announcements condensed the Rockaways to "Rockaway," and the next word was "Babylon." I heard it fairly often, that string of suburban towns, within it the place-names "Rockaway, Babylon."

I was twenty-four years old, and writing plays for broadcast. The era became known as the Golden Age of Television and was characterized by live plays fifty minutes long and not part of a series—over and done with after a single performance. The shows had names like *Kraft Television Theatre, Playhouse 90, Philco Television Playhouse, Studio One, Robert Montgomery Presents*. Live shows, real time, no cutting room, no editing, fluffs galore. If an actor tripped, fell, and went down shouting "Shit," that became a line in your play. It happened. I wrote five plays, three were bought, and two were produced, all for and by *Robert Montgomery Presents*, on NBC. My two that were broadcast were both adaptations of short *New Yorker* fiction by Robert M. Coates. One was a fantasy called "The Man Who Vanished," and that was exactly his problem. He was so downhearted and disappointed by his career and his urban life that he literally dimmed down from time to time, faded. In Studio 8H, the largest at 30 Rockefeller Plaza, the play's sets included many duplicates. For example, the sidewalk, awning, and front door of an apartment building stood adjacent to the identical sidewalk, awning, and front door of an apartment building. Standing under the awning, the man who vanished became dim and then dimmer and dimmer until he was gone altogether. This was achieved by two television cameras, each pointing in an identical way into one of the duplicate sets. As the image with the man in it was faded out, the image without the man in it was faded in. Television technology, 1956. The sets in 8H cost a hundred thousand dollars and were gone forever in the morning. The purchasing power of a hundred thousand dollars in 1956 has become a million dollars at this writing.

Robert Montgomery not only produced the plays but hosted them and sometimes acted in them. Suave and sophisticated, he was good at comedy but equally comfortable in serious drama. He had started on Broadway and gone on to be a durable bright star in Hollywood. When I visited his office, I always felt that I had somehow wandered into the wrong room.

One time, I told him about Penn Station, about the cadenced sound of the Long Island towns, rising through "Rockaway, Babylon," and what a good title that would make. He almost frightened me with his enthusiasm. At least twice, he repeated the names himself. He told me to write a play with that title. Which I meant to do, for a while. But I had trouble thinking up a relevant plot. Moreover, I was developing a sense that as a would-be writer I had entered a realm where I didn't want to stay. I wasn't at ease with directors, casting directors, actors, and all the rest being significant shapers of the finished product. I wanted to make the whole shoe. The kitchen was too full of cooks for me. I wanted to keep my metaphors unmixed.

So twenty-five years went by, it was now 1981, and my sister and brother and parents were all living in Maryland, and what connected us was I-95. Ninety-nine miles south of Princeton and barely into Maryland was a big green sign with bold white letters arranged exactly like this: NORTH EAST RISING SUN.

Every time, I fantasized about that sign. An ode to the illusions of summer. An internment camp from the Second World War. A Shinto shrine. One day on West Forty-third Street, I mentioned the sign to *The New Yorker*'s editor, William Shawn. He knew his way around nutty writers, but was also sensitive to their whims. I proposed going to Maryland to find a story for the title off the sign. Right back, he said, "Yes. Oh, yes." He was romantic, too. And if there was no overlap with the established terrain of another writer, he let you try things on your own. After all, he wasn't paying you, unless he bought the finished piece.

With equal spacing and no punctuation, the sign refers to two towns. Rising Sun, population under three thousand, is seven miles north by northwest of I-95. The town of North East, population about thirty-five hundred, is three miles from I-95 on the other side, at the closed end of a peripheral baylet off the Chesapeake Bay. An English settlement from 1658, North East was where the Susquehannocks camped before Columbus was conceived. Shawnees as well.

I have never followed up. I have just kept driving past the sign. Mr. Shawn thought the project was a good idea. It was not a good idea. It was a good title.

In 1986, there came a third example. Example of what? Of a cart before a horse that wasn't there—a title without a text, just up in the air, a beckoning, beguiling temptation to enter a probable void. I was in Laramie doing research for a book about the geology of Wyoming, and I happened to look up at a bas-relief high on the front of the engineering building at the University of Wyoming. It said, STRIVE ON—THE CONTROL OF NATURE IS WON, NOT GIVEN. The bilateral symmetry in the pertinent four of those words set me off in pursuit of a book to call *The Control of Nature*. In Louisiana, California, Iceland, and Hawaii, I did find that one.

Dams 2020

On October 13, 2020, *The New York Times* printed an item called "Environmentalists and Dam Operators, at War for Years, Start Making Peace," by Brad Plumer. Reading it, I thought about my writing life with dams and dam builders and dam operators and environmentalists—Glen Canyon Dam, Hoover Dam, Anchor Dam, Edwards Dam, Bonneville Dam, Starved Rock Dam, Amoskeag Dam, Bull Shoals Dam—and about the outlook of other people who had been there with me. Holyoke Dam. Hooksett Dam. The dam sites of Dickey-Lincoln. The many nameless dams on rural streams in upstate New York.

The first dam-crazed environmentalist I spent any time with was David Brower, Executive Director of the Sierra Club, later the founder of Friends of the Earth. He died in 2000 but if he could somehow have foreseen the *New York Times* headline about

who had begun his career as a county agent in Wyoming, helping ranchers dam rivulets to make stock ponds and save their animals from dying in drought, not to mention the ranchers' families. Rising through state and federal bureaucracies, he had become the United States Commissioner of Reclamation, head of the unit of the Department of the Interior that built the big western dams— Glen Canyon, Bonneville, Grand Coulee, Flaming Gorge, and so on. Dominy's plans had included a dam or two on the Colorado River within the Grand Canyon, and Brower had attacked him in Congressional hearings. The better to stage a close-up verbal fight, Brower, Dominy, and I went through the Grand Canyon on a neoprene raft past Dominy's dam sites. My daughters were in grade school when the Brower-Dominy book was published. Asked to come to Johnson Park School and describe the book project to the combined second and third grades, I told them about Brower and what dams do to rivers and to the environment of rivers, and I told them about Dominy and the stock ponds saving the animals and also about the big reservoirs that irrigate western valleys and the hydroelectric dams that light whole cities. I did my best to put things the way Brower and Dominy might have. At the end, I called for a vote. Raise your hand if you would be for building new dams. Now raise your hand if you would be against it. Exactly fifty per cent of the children voted one way, and fifty per cent the other way. In this, there seemed to be a pro- phetic message: "Environmentalists and Dam Operators, at War for Years, Start Making Peace."

That was many years ago, when people would have thought "global warming" meant something to do with a ball-top ter- rarium. In decades before that—in the nineteen-twenties, in the Dust Bowl years, and during the hydroelectrification of the Tennessee Valley—the perceived beneficence of dams was high. Opposition was unusual but not unknown. Thoreau, a century earlier, had taken note of the deleterious effect dams were having on migratory fish, and had counselled these anadromous species to "keep a stiff fin" and hope for a better world. But the dichotomy referred to in the *New York Times* headline did not rise to a peak until the last third of the twentieth century, with great battles over the whole range from new dam sites to dam removal. Brower had an undeniable point to make about the identified sites of potential dams. Wherever they are—at Tocks Island in the Delaware River between New Jersey and Pennsylvania, at Dickey and at Lincoln School on the St. John River in northernmost Maine—they never go away. Environmentalists might win battles against the construction of dams, as they did at those places, but the sites would be there forever.

After a ceremonial event in Humboldt County, California, Brower introduced me to George Hartzog, Director of the National Park Service. Waiting to board an airplane, Hartzog talked fishing. This led to interviews, correspondence, and the cold tailwaters of Bull Shoals Dam on the White River of northern Arkansas, where we caught a slew of stocked trout on canned corn, one kernel per trout. Our campsite was a short distance below the dam. Morning, evening, across the day, the river was erratic there. To me, it seemed "as natural as a city street."

> The White River grows toward the end of the day. Around 5:30 P.M., people start turning on lights, heating up ovens, and frying pork chops in Fayetteville, Little Rock, Mountain

Home, Memphis. The river rises. More people, more pork chops—the river goes on rising. Turbines spin in Bull Shoals Dam. The peak comes when a million pork chops are sizzling all at once and the river is so high it flows around the trunks of trees. Then it starts going down. While Arkansas sleeps, the river goes down so far that the trout have to know where to go to survive. At 6 A.M., a small creek is running through the riverbed, viscous with trout. Then people start getting up in Fayetteville, Little Rock, Mountain Home, and Memphis. The fatback hits the frying pans. Up comes the river, cold, clear, fast, and green.

The dam in Dickey, Maine, on the St. John River, was going to do that. A mile and three-quarters wide, it was to be more than three hundred feet high, and it would flood the boreal forest of Maine for fifty-seven miles, with a lake surface exceeding eighty-eight thousand acres. That's a lot of bear fat. The dam at Dickey would make the peaking power, and in doing so would release so much water that another dam—at Lincoln School, eleven miles downstream—was needed to catch it and avert disaster. Meanwhile, the fifty-seven-mile lake behind the Dickey Dam would fluctuate with season and weather. When the lake shrank to a predicted "minimum pool," thirty thousand acres would emerge as a muckland galactic with stumps.

That scenario was what disgusted environmentalists, and made them gag when hydropower was described as "clean." A month after ice-out in 1975, I went down the St. John with seven of them—in four canoes, a hundred and some miles to the Canadian border from a small lake near the headwaters—and in the

piece I wrote afterward, called "The Keel of Lake Dickey," I struggled to preserve whatever status I had as an unbiased journalistic
observer. Describing the scene at Dickey, however, where the dam
would be nearly two miles wide, and where we looked up from
the river imagining its crest more than three hundred vertical feet
above us, I lost my journalistic cool, lost all cool, not for the first
time, and fulminated for three or four pages about the intrusions
and deceptions of hydro-dams, and

> an apparent belief that it is the right of people to have all
> the electric power they can afford to buy, with the subsidi-
> ary right of squandering it when and how they please and of
> buying it at the same rate at any time of day. We throw away
> more power than a Dickey Dam could ever give us, by ten
> times ten times ten. We throw it away in kilowatt-years. And
> anyone who would do that would throw away a river.

The dawn and dusk writhing of rivers below power dams
was repeated around the world, because—all battery technology
notwithstanding—electricity's overwhelming sell-by date is the
moment it is made. Firing up a plant with steam-driven turbines
is a plodding way to get to that moment, so hydro was the obvious
choice to deal with erratic demand and deliver "peaking power."
Release water to fall into turbines and electricity travels to some
millions of stoves at the speed of light. The farther the water fell,
the more electricity it made. And this had led to something called
pumped storage. Three years before the Dickey-Lincoln proposal,
New York's Consolidated Edison Company, having found an
ideal location on Storm King Mountain, on the Hudson River just

above West Point, proposed to pump river water up the mountain, hold it there in a reservoir, and release it at times and in amounts chosen ad hoc by Con Edison, to fall to turbines set in a massive cut in the lower face of the mountain. This resulted in eyeball-to-eyeball rage between environmentalists and Con Edison. The environmentalists sued in federal court. At this writing, sixty years later, there is no pumped storage at Storm King.

In the same era, a pumped-storage plant was built at Ludington, Michigan, with Lake Michigan as one reservoir and a depression up a sand dune the other. That depression, actually, holds twenty-seven billion gallons of water, and the Ludington plant, as it opened for business in the nineteen-seventies, was the largest pumped-storage facility in the world. Because sand is porous and permeable, the reservoir's bottom was lined with asphalt and clay. Through penstocks, its water runs downdune three hundred and sixty-three vertical feet to the turbines below. In fewer than two minutes, more than eighteen hundred megawatts spread through Michigan and beyond.

In New Jersey, meanwhile (as mentioned earlier, in "Walking the Province Line"), the U.S. Army Corps of Engineers was proposing pumped storage at Sunfish Pond on the Appalachian Trail, twelve hundred vertical feet above the Delaware River. Sunfish Pond is a natural feature gouged out in the Pleistocene by the continental ice sheet that covered New England and New York and was a mile thick over New Jersey down to a terminal moraine about thirty miles south of Sunfish Pond. The Corps planned to deepen, widen, and lengthen the pond, otherwise preserving it in its natural state. Sunfish Pond put the environmental movement on greased ball bearings. Environmentalists, in federal court, killed the project.

In 1985, after eight years of construction, a pumped-storage plant even larger than Michigan's began emitting power beside an Appalachian creek in Virginia, very close to the West Virginia border. Officially the Bath County Pumped Storage Station, it was billed as "the largest battery in the world." In a sense it was, with twelve hundred and sixty vertical feet of generating head, and a water-storage capacity that could be turned into twenty-four thousand megawatt-hours. At this writing, thirty-five years later, there are forty-three pumped-storage plants in the United States and a number approaching three hundred in the world.

If environmentalists needed a talisman, they had one in Anchor Dam, in the Bighorn Basin, in Wyoming. Completed in 1960, a thin-arch concrete structure nearly six hundred feet wide and two hundred high, it was built over a creek bed and was designed to impound twenty-one million five hundred thousand cubic meters of water. I went there in the nineteen-eighties with David Love, of the United States Geological Survey. The dam was a quarter-century old and glistened like new on both sides. Whatever the reservoir took in, it quickly let go, without help from the Bureau of Reclamation. The dam had impounded essentially nothing. The water drains away through the rock beneath the dam, which, variously, is sandstone and dolomite. The sandstone, as noted, is porous and permeable. Dolomite is soluble in water. You paid for the dam.

In my most poignant memories of dams, that one ranks right up there with Edwards, Bonneville, and Glen Canyon. Standing with Dave Brower in a chamber deep inside Glen Canyon Dam, I all but needed an umbrella against the water dripping into the hollows of the dam from the reservoir behind it known as Lake Powell. A concrete arch seven hundred feet high and fifteen hundred wide, it is one of fifteen dams in the Colorado River and was only three years old when we were inside it. There was zero danger of its coming apart. At some point in eternity, there would be—one drip at a time.

The most memorable aspect of Bonneville was not so much the theater seats and plate-glass windows deep inside the structure, where you could watch, as they swam by, some portion of the five million American shad that come up the Columbia River in spring, but the people outside who were fishing for them in the tailrace rapids. Only in the open-air Greenmarket at Flatbush and Atlantic in Brooklyn had I ever seen as rich a cross-section of the peoples of the earth in one place. The common chord in their uncountable languages was excitement. Five million shad! I tied on a three-sixteenths-ounce chartreuse dart and flipped it into a foam-lined eddy.

Edwards Dam, on the Kennebec River in Augusta, Maine, was nine hundred feet from bank to bank. It was built in 1837, and its removal—on the first of July, 1999—symbolized the philosophical distance that had developed in the late twentieth century between dam operators and environmentalists. It was also the first big dam in a major American river to be ordered out of existence by the federal government, setting a precedent for dam removal after dam removal in all parts of the country. Edwards Dam was prepared for destruction in such a way that a series of scoops by a Caterpillar 345 backhoe with a four-yard bucket could eat away a gravel plug at one end, releasing the elevated water upstream. Bunting adorned the event. National television. Reporters from cities in four time zones. In something called the Tree-Free Parking Lot, on the left bank of the river, more than a thousand environmentalists gathered. Champagne toasts—to a victory that would invert itself and become a rapprochement in twenty years. Bruce Babbitt, the Secretary of the Interior, made a speech. Angus King, the Governor of Maine, made a speech. Migratory fish—alewives, American shad, Atlantic sturgeon, Atlantic salmon—were, in effect, told that they would no longer have to keep a stiff fin and hope for a better world. I scribbled notes for a piece called "Farewell to the Nineteenth Century." At last, the backhoe made its moves and water thundered through the breach. Moments beforehand, in the broad river pool below the dam, an Atlantic salmon leaped so high it cleared the surface by a couple of feet, and hung there, as if on cue.

Breaking Away

I have written stories drawn from my mother's life and my father's life ("Silk Parachute," "The Patch"), each of which, in book form, was the title piece of a miscellaneous collection, but I have never undertaken a biography of either. Some time ago, and not long after my mother's death at the age of one hundred, I found among her possessions a brief manuscript titled "Mary's Story." It seemed to have been written when she was in her upper eighties, and her extraordinary penmanship was still as clear and readable as Times Roman. With her children and grandchildren in mind, she somehow persuaded my father to join her in the endeavor. After

"Mary's Story," a fresh page was titled "Mickey's Story," and his text began with this sentence:

> I was born at 119 Forest Avenue in Youngstown, Ohio, in a little four room house with no indoor facilities whatsoever, two rooms downstairs and two up.

"Mickey's Story" not only began but also ended with that sentence. There was, is, will be no more from him. She tried. Meanwhile, "Mary's Story," although just a beginning itself, threw shafts of light into many themes, from the education of women in her time and place to the control parenting of a father with a son, who did not prosper in the classroom, and four bright daughters. Whatever I may once have contemplated about growing these stories into a long composition of my own is not going to happen now. I will leave that to my own four bright daughters, all professors—Sarah, an art historian; Laura, an artist photographer; Jenny and Martha, the two novelists (Jenny also teaches translation and translates Italian fact and fiction into English). If that isn't enough to do better than I ever could with their paternal grandparents' stories, maybe their children can help.

Meanwhile, I will reproduce my mother's short manuscript, feeling free to make it even shorter, and free also to toss in a comment here and there in brackets.

MARY'S STORY

> I was born in Lansdowne, Pa., a suburb of Philadelphia, on August 7th, 1897. I was the third of five children. Laura was 3½, and my only brother was 17 months older than I. He was

very, very sick as a baby and not expected to live. So I was told that I walked before he did; but being older, he talked first. We started kindergarten together and went on in the same class, graduating together. I don't remember it, but they said I fought with other children if they picked on my brother because he was slower doing things. I was a good student and he was a poor one. So when we were given our report cards to take home to be signed by a parent, he didn't want to be scolded so wouldn't let me show mine at home until the school was demanding their return. I had good grades and of course wanted to show them.

[When I was at Princeton High School, she asked incessantly why I had no schoolwork to do at home. Actually, I brought books home and put them under my bed before going out back to shoot baskets under a lightbulb I had hung from the roof.]

Our high school was easy—no stimulus, and I never had to bring my homework home. In those days pupils "skipped a grade" in those circumstances. My father wouldn't allow me to be skipped, because then I would have been a year ahead of my older brother. So I suppose my father felt guilty. Anyway, he decided to teach me French. I had a first-year French book, and was questioned a bit, and then assigned the next chapter for homework. There was a paragraph in French to translate into English, and a longer paragraph in English to translate into French. Very simple, and I enjoyed it. But the next year Daddy couldn't take me any further and he sent me in to the University of Pennsylvania for second-year French with graduate students. I didn't mind it, but I always hated being different. I couldn't do what the others might be doing after school that day (once a week) and I couldn't explain why I was going. I just knew I had to do what my father wanted me to do. The "bait" he held out was that after college he would send me to France for a year. So I went to the University for two years, I think. Even a summer school one year. The bait that time was a season pass for the University swimming pool. No one had private pools then, so my only place to swim was when we went to the Ocean. I loved the gym pool, altho' I had no one to use it with me.

[Her father had graduated from the University of Pennsylvania at the age of nineteen. His first name was John, he was called Will, and his full name was John Williamson Ziegler.]

Daddy was a quiet man, very bright, very interested in his business, his family, his church.

[His business was publishing. He was second-in-command of the John C. Winston Company, "Book and Bible Publishers," which claimed to hustle more Bibles than any other company in the world. His church was Methodist. His wife, my grandmother, was a Quaker.]

I never heard him swear. But we all knew that he was the head of the house. A couple of times I remember rebelling at having to go to church as well as Sunday school. Each time when I stayed home, he had something nice planned for us in the afternoon, and he would say "No, Mary, thee can't go. Thee wasn't well enough for church this morning." So—we learned—and generally did what we were supposed to.

[My mother and her sister Rachel spoke Plain Speech to each other as long as both lived. Until my mother was somewhere in her nineties, she thoroughly proofread the galleys of every one of my books. She once queried me about my various uses and occasional lowercase spelling of "God."]

After I had gone to the University for several courses, Daddy had another bright idea. (Maybe he had known it all along.) He talked to the University and the word was that if I passed a test on first-year French they would give me credit. Then I would have 20 hours credit and could enter college as a sophomore deficient in ten credits, which, with one summer school I could easily make up, graduate in three years, and then he would send me to France to study for a year.

[A world war and a pandemic would be waiting at the far end of college. When she taught French in a Cleveland high school while my father was in medical school at Western Reserve, she had never been to France. If you haven't seen *Breaking Away*, see *Breaking Away*.]

So—in 1915 I graduated from High School, and in September I left for Oberlin. I could have gone to Swarthmore or Bryn Mawr or the University of Pennsylvania, but would have been a day student, and I wanted campus life. So I went to Oberlin, and later on both Ruth and Rachel started there. I had a job drying dishes at Churchill, my dormitory. I resented that without ever saying so—again it was because I always hated to be different. The other girls did not work, just me. However, looking back, I realize that my job helped me to know Mickey. He was waiting table at Churchill. One boy's job was to wash dishes, and I dried them. There was laughing and joking in the kitchen after meals, and we got well acquainted. There were only twelve girls at Churchill, but 12 more from a small dormitory across the street, and 12 or 15 more students ate there. After supper, we would play games, or someone would play the piano, etc. At 7:30 everyone had to leave, and we had to go upstairs and be quiet for study until 9:30 or 9:40. Then there was noise and laughter as we got ready for bed—lights out at ten o'clock.

That's how Mickey and I got to know and like each other. In the spring came the O Club banquet—a party only for men who had earned a letter in some sport. One evening as we girls were going upstairs to study, Mickey asked me if I would go with him. I was so thrilled I said I didn't remember going up any more steps! I was a sophomore but really only a first year student. He was a Junior, and as someone wrote to one of my sisters, "Mary, I understand, is going with Oberlin's hero." She didn't just mean to the banquet. By that time we were together quite a lot.

[Mickey was a three-sport athlete, best known beyond Oberlin for his achievements in basketball.]

Mickey's course required one Summer School, and I had to stay to make up my missing credits. All girls moved to the big dorm, Talcott Hall, and all men ate there. So that's where we had lots of time together. Long walks all over Oberlin, etc.

Oberlin would not allow fraternities, but there were some secret ones. All Mickey's athletic friends had joined, and Mickey was asked to join, but had held off till after graduation at his mother's request. That summer after his Junior year the Dean found out about the fraternities and all the students who were members were expelled. That meant practically the whole football team. Of course it was a disastrous season for football. Ohio State beat Oberlin 128–0. Mickey was the basketball captain and should never have played football, but he tried to help. He was injured—was on crutches well into the basketball season, which was a shame.

In April of that year 1917, war broke out. All Seniors were given leave to enlist, and still be graduated. Mickey joined the Youngstown hospital Unit. They hadn't left Youngstown by June, so he came back for a week to graduate. I was a Junior, and at Oberlin Juniors were very much a part of the graduation events. That was one of the happiest weeks of my life.

[The three-page "Mary's Story" ends there.]

The Eunuch of Talcott Hall

On Christmas Eves in the nineteen-thirties, there would be a ho ho ho in the dark outside our door, on Maple Street in Princeton, and we would open it to admit Santa Claus. In he came—all red, white, and beard; everything but the creosote. He carried a big sack full of presents. He smelled faintly, but not of reindeer. More like a hospital. He was yuley, merry, and jolly as all hell, redolent of tidings of great joy. When I was seven, my brother, Roemer, was thirteen. After Santa Claus handed him a present, Roemer said, "Thank you, Dr. Tenney."

Luman Tenney, M.D., a psychiatrist, was a colleague of my father on the medical staff of Princeton University. He lived with his family beside the pond at Grovers Mill, three miles from the Princeton campus. Eight weeks before that Christmas, invading Martians had landed in considerable numbers beside the pond at Grovers Mill. At least thousands of people thought so as they listened to CBS radio's version of H. G. Wells's *The War of the Worlds*, the news-like broadcast that put the Martians at the pond and was so realistic that it is assigned in psych courses to this day. Never mind that the aliens landed on Mischief Night, the eve of Halloween. Clearly, they were no match for Santa Claus, who, when he showed up on Christmas Eve, was in no way the worse for wear.

Dr. Tenney was a man of modest height, trim, chunky, athletic. The twinkle in his eyes was no act. It signalled a great sense of humor. He had known my parents for more than two decades, since the three of them were students together at Oberlin, the first co-educational college in the United States (1833). Dr. Tenney had been born in Oberlin. Like my father, he was trained as a physician at Western Reserve, in Cleveland. He once told me that as an Oberlin student he had been "the eunuch of Talcott Hall," the women's dorm. I must have been in high school by then if he thought I would understand what he meant. I thought he had a part in a play. Evidently, he had had some sort of student employment there, with a job description he was prone to escalate.

By January after the Martians landed, the pond at Grovers Mill was frozen so firmly that Dr. Tenney could drive on it in his Ford Coupe. He tied a long rope to the rear bumper, as he did winter after winter, and hauled us around on our sleds—"us" being me, my brother, my sister, and, as they became old enough, his two sons, all taking turns with the rope. One time, a wheel went through the ice, but that was rare. Dr. Tenney was a Martian and a half.

Hyperlincs, the Gettysburg Addresses,
or the Shot Heard Round the Web

This was meant to be the first salvo in a war on hyperlinks:

Four score and seven years ago (https://newsfeed.time.com
/2010/11/19/seven-score-and-seven-years-ago-what-you-dont
-know) our fathers brought forth on this continent (https://www
.mapsofworld.com/north-america/), a new nation (https://www
.georgewashingtoninauguralbuttons.com/the-first-mapofthe-united
-states/), conceived in Liberty, and dedicated to the proposition
that all men are created equal (https://www.logcabinsyrups.com/)
(https://www.knobcreek.com/).

Now we are engaged in a great civil war (https://www.history
.com/topics/american-civil-war), testing whether that nation, or
any nation so conceived and so dedicated, can long endure. We
are met on a great battle-field of that war (https://www.historynet
.com/battle-of-gettysburg). We have come to dedicate a portion
of that field (https://www.google.com/search?source=univ&tbm
=isch&q=gettysburg+battlefield+map&sa=X&ved=) as (https://
www.taqz/noisill/stephendouglas.org) (https://www.copperpenny
/cyprusemine.com) (https://wysiwyg.masodixie.gov) (https://
www.qwertyuiop[]@ . . . : . . .)

Time passed. I waved a white flag.

Not That One

Edward Abbey was a walking Profile subject. In 1972, I came close to acting on that fact, but in the ensuing years never got to it, as with all the other story ideas in this reminiscent montage. Abbey came to Princeton as a guest speaker in a colloquium series called "On Wilderness," organized by two young physicists, Rob Socolow and Hal Feiveson, who described themselves and a number of colleagues as the Center for Environmental Studies. The colloquia were open to the public, and the public came—townspeople, tennis shoes—crowding a large living room also occupied by some interested students and faculty. These were among the harbingers of environmentalism in an academic curriculum, of what evolved some years later into Princeton's Department of Ecology and Evolutionary Biology.

Four years earlier, Abbey had published *Desert Solitaire*, a nonfiction rumination about his time as a seasonal ranger at Arches National Monument, in Utah. The book is full of anarchism and vitriol with regard to land use, not to mention Abbey's signature bluntness and wry, dry humor. This was a writer who wrote his own last words long before the day came when he might have said them. In a desert location still unknown, friends who buried him set a rock by the grave and scratched on it Abbey's last words: "No comment."

At the Princeton colloquium, in Stevenson Hall, Abbey sat in a large upholstered armchair, his long legs stretched out, his look dark and handsome, his cowboy boots showing wear. He had come a long way from Home, Pennsylvania, where he grew up. His home at the time was near Tucson. The Center for Environmental Studies had entitled his appearance "The Modern Battle of the Wilderness," and nearly all of what he said was in thoughtful response to questions from the floor. Afterward, I volunteered to show him around Princeton, it being my home town. He accepted readily, and in the morning I turned up at the university's guesthouse, and off we went. For several hours, we walked all over the campus and through Princeton's gradational neighborhoods. Loose, lanky, in his Western hat and boots, emitting that quiet humor, he was one likable guy. But that memorable walk is not the most memorable item that has lingered from Abbey's visit. Most of the questions asked by the crowd in Stevenson Hall of course had to do with *Desert Solitaire*, including one from a woman who appeared to be at least Abbey's age, which was forty-five. She brought up an "experiment" he describes in the book—conducted outside his house trailer in Utah—when he "volunteered" a passing rabbit as the experimentee. He picked up a rock, fired it at the rabbit, and brained it on the spot. The woman in Princeton said to him, "How could you do that? How could you be so cruel? How could you . . ." and so forth. She really lit into him. Sitting back in the upholstered armchair with his legs at full stretch, one boot across the other, he seemed to be aiming through a kind of gun sight formed by his toes. There was a long silence—Abbey silent, everyone in the room silent. And more silence. Finally, Abbey said, "I won't do it again." Muted laughter rippled here and there. And again Abbey fell silent, for an even longer time, and then he said, "Not to that rabbit."

Night Watchman

In June, 1948, when I graduated from Princeton High School, I already had a job, as a night watchman at the Institute for Advanced Study, on the far side of town. All kinds of people assumed that the Institute was part of Princeton University, which it wasn't and isn't. My job was not actually inside the Institute's one completed building, but outside, in the back, where two smaller and bilaterally symmetrical buildings were under construction. Halfway between them was a pinewood-and-tarpaper shack, where foremen presided by day and watchmen at night, protecting bricks, lumber, reinforcing rods, nails, wood screws, and double-point staples from thieves who would come to take them. There was no shortage of thieves.

My weapon was a billy club—a ball of lead wrapped in leather with a nine-inch stem and a loop handle. It was the only weapon, if you did not include the flashlight. I would include the flashlight. Its beam could warn a ship at sea, intimidate an actor, shine brighter than the headlight of a locomotive. Mostly, I was just there, passing time, expecting events that were not happening. In fair weather, I climbed up onto the flat roof of the construction shack, and lay there, staring at the rear elevation of the Institute's main building, Fuld Hall. It was only nine years old—dedicated in 1939—and nine years younger than the Institute itself, founded in 1930. Institute mathematicians, during those nine years, worked in a space on the Princeton campus, giving rise to the flattering myth that the Institute was part of the university. How flattering? Think Albert Einstein.

Night watchmen guarding rebars don't mix with the occupants of a Fuld Hall. I had never heard of most of them anyway. The director's name was J. Robert Oppenheimer. He lived at the far end of the Institute's front lawn in a house that is, in part, the oldest in Princeton. Einstein lived on Mercer Street a mile away, and walked to work. Arnold Toynbee was at the Institute in 1948, in the School of Historical Studies. Among the visiting professors in the School of Mathematics were Aage Bohr, Harald Bohr, and Niels Bohr. John von Neumann had been there from the outset. By 1948, Kurt Gödel, Oswald Veblen, and Hermann Weyl were there, too. Freeman Dyson, on the natural-sciences faculty from 1953 to 2020, was a new Fellow at the Institute in 1948. The professors had no students, or, at least, did not teach classes. They had been drawn to the Institute for Advanced Study to advance their own research. I knew that much.

Fuld Hall was dark at night, no permanent lighting. I just stared at it, in moonlight, starlight, rain. My field of vision went around both ends and outward. When thieves came, I could not see them coming, because they approached very slowly, in pickups, with the headlights off. They came all the way down Olden Lane with headlights off. They crept onto the gravel parking lot at the east end of Fuld Hall. It was a big parking lot covered with sharp-sided diabase gravel. The ever-so-slowly creeping tires of the pickups made clear sound on the gravel. My doorbell. With the billy club in one hand, the flashlight in the other, I moved up the lawn toward the building, stood in the darkness, and waited. I heard small sounds—a click, a ping, a scrape, and footsteps.

As it happens, I am a lot smaller than most night watchmen. A point guard, not a security guard. And a very short point guard at that. In moonlight, I got behind a bush. As the footsteps moved toward the rebars, sometimes with a visible figure attached, I raised the flashlight above my head as high as I could reach and turned it on. In the same instant, I growled a noise as guttural and menacing as my voice could produce, intending a message to the thief that a six-six thug with a blinding light was about to kill him.

It worked. So did I—for the George A. Fuller construction company. And I never used the billy club.

Other nights in the wee hours, headlights would appear far up Olden Lane and a car would come barrelling toward the Institute, reach the parking lot, and skid to a stop on the gravel. A door would open and slam shut. The driver would run to the building and go inside. Moments later, a light would appear in an upstairs window, to burn for the rest of the night. Whoever it was had had an idea.

George Recker and Dr. Dick

McKenzie River, in McKenzie boats, in Oregon with Dr. Dick. Worthy of a tome, Lenox Dick. Author of *Experience the World of Shad Fishing* (Frank Amato Publications, Portland, 1996). Author of *The Art and Science of Fly Fishing* (Winchester Press, 1972). His medical practice is in Portland, and he lives on the Columbia River in Vancouver, Washington. When he's hungry for one of five million migrating shad, he walks down his lawn to the river with his fly rod.

Now on the McKenzie on June 21, 2006, he is rowing his own boat, his own McKenzie River rhombus, with its narrow transom, its rocker bottom meant for white water. We're getting plenty of that. It requires a first-class five-star river boatman, a rank Dr. Dick has long since given himself and is not about to relinquish at the age of ninety. This storied tributary of the Willamette, falling out of the Cascade Range in the southern part of the state, is one of America's great trout rivers, and that's what we're out here to catch. Dr. Dick has Roger Bachman, of Portland, with him. They have been fishing together since 1492. Roger is somewhat younger. Their friend the author Jessica Maxwell, of Eugene, young by my standards let alone theirs, is in the other boat with me and George Recker, a professional fishing guide. This river is no chalk stream. With its haystacks and standing waves and boulderfield eddies below pools of fast flat water, its rhythmic curves, it has the shape of a downhill ski run. Lenox Dick may be ninety, but he rows that boat as if he's in a regatta, and is often far ahead.

I have been with him on other rivers. He has an old cabin on the left bank of the Deschutes. A road runs up the right bank from Maupin, but there is no road anywhere near the left. He parks on the right bank and launches his boat, several hundred yards downstream of the cabin because there's no closer place to park. The first time I did this with him, the Deschutes was vicious wall to wall. Hard, fast, rolling current. Tall, rangy, confident— a medical missionary in Africa years before—Lenox was nonetheless eighty-six at the time. I was only seventy-one, and I thought I might fare better in that current than he would. Moreover, I was frightened out of my mind. I said, "Len, why not let me do the rowing?"

"You would screw it up!" he said, and he started off, aiming upriver at forty-five degrees. The river was only two or three hundred feet wide, but the crossing proceeded slowly because we were moving southwest and northwest at the same time. My heart was beating between my teeth. The left bank was almost uniformly high and steep there but Len hit a spot where a gully had worn down. The next day we crossed the river twice, just to go to Maupin and buy more flies. Thanks to his instructions and suggestions, I caught five rainbows, inspiring me to write:

> A day or two later, he left for Wyoming to fish the Green River. In three weeks, he was off to Iceland in pursuit of Atlantic salmon. Fish or no fish, when I grow up I want to be like him.

When Len was eighty-eight, we started down the John Day. Roger Bachman was aboard, Len rowing us in his boat. Farther east, and like the Deschutes, the John Day is a north-flowing tributary of the Columbia River. Known for its bass, it doesn't have the world-class reputation the Deschutes has for its steelhead and trout. Scarcely a mile from launch, we received an omen from John Day. Len ran up on a boulder in the middle of the river. Stuck fast, we rocked back and forth and side to side and Len scraped rock with the oars. We were there quite a while. Gradually our commotion inched the boat off the boulder. And soon we heard a rumble of thunder, and sooner still another. We hadn't gone five miles when we decided to make camp early. Lightning was all over the place and rain with it. Thunderstorms don't last

forever. Under a tarp, just sit and wait. And wait. And wait forever, it seemed. More rain. Who expects rain at this time of year
in eastern Oregon? The shade of John Day, evidently. All-night
rain. Wearing waders, wading boots, waterproof jackets, there was
no point in taking anything off. Just lie on the ground with the
tarp, in water streaming by. With daylight, we bailed out the boat,
went on to the next bridge, and managed the recovery of the car. In
a lifetime of sleeping some hundreds of nights on the ground, that
for me was the last one. To date.

And now, two years later, we're on the McKenzie River with
the professional guide George Recker, and we have had our lunch:
the ten-inch trout we were catching this morning. George prepared them, and grilled them naked. Skinless. After beheading
each one, he pinched it with his thumbs and forefingers at the pec-
toral fins and flipped it over-end with a powerful snap. The body
popped out of the skin, looking less like a fish than a frankfurter.

Back on the river, Recker, with little choice, followed Dr. Dick
downstream. As we fell farther behind, George became concerned
about his ninety-year-old client. In case of trouble, shouts would
not be heard. And there soon arose a situation of real alarm. At the
far end of a long right-bending curve, the river was really wild. We
could make out in the distance its snapping white jaws. Dr. Dick
was rowing blithely toward the jaws. George reached into his kit.
He removed a miniature trumpet, stunningly beautiful, in silver
and gold. Also employed as a professor of music at the University
of Oregon, George Recker the professional fishing guide had been
first trumpet for operas at the Kennedy Center, in Washington.
He lifted the miniature trumpet to his lips and produced a long
clear note that may have reached the moon. It sent Dr. Dick to
the riverbank.

Dinners with Henry Luce

Henry Luce, co-founder of *Time: The Weekly Newsmagazine*, would try to get to know new writers by inviting them to dinner at his New York apartment. At least, he was doing that when I was a new writer, thirty-four years after the founding, when Luce was living for the most part in Arizona and was not a presence in the magazine's offices. I went to two of those dinners, each time seated with some eleven other writers at a long table, as if Leonardo da Vinci were on hand, too. Luce asked questions, going around the table from face to face for answers. One such dinner, in the summer of 1960, occurred after Richard Nixon had won the Republican nomination for President and before he made his choice of a candidate for Vice-President. Two of us—Jesse Birnbaum and I—sat side by side at one end of the table, Luce alone at the other end. He was sixty-two but looked and seemed older. In his voice was the scratch of antiquity. After several rounds of questions, my attention span collapsed, a general tendency in my psychological makeup that I am shy to acknowledge. There came a question that I failed to hear, and down the right side of the table five answers were given, all of which bypassed whatever daydream I was having. The substance of the question was who did the young writers think Nixon's choice would be. Jesse Birnbaum was on my left, so I was number six in line. The fog lifted suddenly when, looking down the table, I saw five people on either side and Luce at the far end looking at me expectantly—at me, clueless and catatonic. Jesse Birnbaum saved me by almost inaudibly whispering, "Henry Cabot Lodge."

"Henry Cabot Lodge!" I said, with conviction.

At the other dinner, Luce's questions were more personal than political. He had gone around the table two or three times when he asked, in effect—I forget how he put it—What is your religion? Luce had credentials in religion. His father was a Presbyterian missionary in China, where Luce was born in 1898. He had attended the China Inland Mission School, in Chefoo, and now he looked down the table for answers to his question. A variety of faiths were mentioned one after another, until all eyes turned to John Alexander Skow. Known to most of us as Jack, he was never unforthcoming. His tone was always gentle, and he was afraid of nothing. In answer to Luce's question, he said, "Atheist anticlerical."

"Wha-wha-wha-what did you say?" said Luce.

"Atheist anticlerical."

Luce became a captive. From that point forward, the evening was composed of nothing but Luce and Skow. While the two of them wrapped each other in rhetoric, the rest of us might as well have crept away.

Bourbon and Bing Cherries

After I wrote a book called *Oranges*, which was about oranges, it caused enduring wonderment in the book press, the inference being that the author of anything like that must be substantially weird. "He wrote a whole book about oranges" has been the most

repeated line, with the word "whole" all but printed in orange ital-
ics. "He wrote a whole book about oranges, his favorite fruit" is an
analytical variation, though contrary to fact. My favorite fruit is
the Bing cherry. And my favorite whiskey is not spelled "whisky"
and happens not to be single-malt Scotch, the subject of a study
that I wrote called "Josie's Well," which is part of a collection
called *Pieces of the Frame*. I didn't need all the diagnostic wonderment to become sane enough not to write about Bing cherries or
bourbon. Who wants to be typecast?

As I wrote in a foreword to a paperback edition published in
London years ago, the origin of oranges as, for me, a subject for a
piece of writing began in New York's Pennsylvania Station in the
nineteen-sixties. A machine in one corner of the train room split
and squeezed oranges. They rolled down a chute and were pressed
against a blade. Then the two halves went in separate directions
to be cupped and squeezed. The juice fell into a pitcher. You paid
dearly for the product.

I was a frequent commuter then, scarcely thirty, and I stopped
at the machine almost every day. From late autumn and on
through winter and spring I noticed a gradual deepening of the
color of the expressed juice. December was pale cadmium, April
marigold, and June a Persian orange. One day, I happened onto
an ad in a magazine, paid for by the Florida Citrus Commission,
picturing four oranges that to me looked identical but had varying
names: Hamlin, Parson Brown, the Washington Navel Orange,
the Late Orange of Valencia. How did they differ from one another? I didn't linger over the question. I had to get to work.

As a new staff writer for *The New Yorker*—in search of topics
and making lists—I thought of the machine in Penn Station, and

the four oranges in the ad. While mentioning a number of story possibilities to William Shawn, the magazine's editor, I uttered the single word "oranges?"

He answered right back. He always answered quickly. It seemed impossible to propose any subject to him that he had not thought about before you had. When he turned down an idea, he was usually protecting the interests of some writer whose name would never be mentioned. "No. I'm very sorry. No," he would say typically, his voice so light it fell like mist. To my question about oranges, though, he said, "Yes. Oh, my, yes."

I intended only some hundreds of words, a few pages in the magazine. On the Ridge—the slightly elevated spine of Florida—I began by flying around in the helicopter of a citrus nurseryman and learning the lore of bud unions. Citrus does not come true from seed. If you plant an orange seed, a grapefruit might spring up. If you plant a seed of that grapefruit, you might get a bitter lemon. With a graft, however, what you saw was what you got. Scion and rootstock were joined at the bud union.

I had moved on to growers and pickers—still on course for that short piece—when someone remarked to me that if I was going to write about oranges I should visit the University of Florida's Citrus Experiment Station, in Lake Alfred.

It was late March and the Valencias, in their overlapping cycle, were in fruit and in bloom, a phenomenon of this tree, which blossoms fourteen months before the fruit is picked, with the beautiful result that a Valencia tree in spring is under a snowy veil punctuated by spots of bright orange against an evergreen field of dark leaves. Valencias were half of Florida's annual crop. The university's experiment station was a couple of buff, squarish buildings that stood alone, deep within a Valencian forest. You went up a long lane through the groves to find it. When you stepped out and walked through the door, your short article turned into a book.

Some dozens of people in there had doctorates in oranges. Many of them were wearing lab coats of the sort issued at a general hospital. They were working on citrus metabolism, on post-harvest diseases. In a chamber that functioned much like a heart-lung machine, oranges wired to sensors were breathing in oxygen and exhaling carbon dioxide, as oranges do until they die. They are long off the tree when they stop breathing. Dr. William Grierson, looking lonely, had a knight's broken lance over his door, which he said he had splintered in defense of fresh fruit, most of which was disappearing in a frozen sea of concentrate (canned, concentrated juice, add water). In the library of the experiment station were a hundred thousand titles on citrus—scientific papers, mainly, but also six thousand books. They crossed a distinguished spectrum from Philip C. Reece and J. F. L. Childs's *Character Differences in Seedlings of the Persian Lime* to Samuel Tolkowsky's monumental *Hesperides: A History of the Culture and Use of Citrus Fruits* and—from several centuries earlier—Giovanni Battista Ferrari's *Hesperides, or Four Books on the Culture and Use of the Golden Apples*. Some of these I took outside and read under trees. I learned that citrus was born in East Asia, migrated westward with civilization, and traversed North Africa with the rise of Islam. There were no oranges in the Holy Land when Christ was alive. Those oranges on the table in various Last Suppers were oranges of Renaissance Italy. Columbus himself brought the first citrus to the New World.

The idea for "Josie's Well" as subject and title of a piece of writing developed in a bathtub in the Hebrides. Our family stayed there for some months in early 1967, living on a croft, our older daughters enrolled in the island school, while I interviewed people and gathered experience on the ancestral island in preparation for a long piece of writing. The whisky was incidental, a variety of single malts—Talisker, Laphroaig, Glenlivet, Macallan—in sipping jiggers at the side of the tub after long days hiking in sequences of sunshine and cold misty rain.

Proofs aside, why the strong taste of island whiskies? Why the mild elegance of the whiskies of Speyside? Why did Laphroaig suggest thick-sliced bacon? In Speyside, on Islay, on Skye, I later interviewed the distillers, including Captain Smith Grant, whose artesian spring, called Josie's Well, was out in the middle of a field of oats near Ballindalloch, Banffshire, and was providing thirty-five hundred gallons an hour to the stills of The Glenlivet.

I prefer bourbon. Admitting it is painful. Disloyalty to ancestors often is. But facts are facts. The single-malt Scotches are for birthdays. Bourbon is for the barricades. The closest I ever came to forsaking my principles—the literary creed that one kind of whiskey is enough for one writing lifetime—came in 2004, when I was working on an unrelated story in Kentucky and had a weekend to kill on my own. I just drove aimlessly around the center of the state. Well, not altogether aimlessly. As a quotidian sipper of bourbon, I gravitated to distilleries, just to see their settings and what they looked like, the possibility of a piece on bourbon now not so far back in my mind. In a park in Bardstown, Kentucky, Stephen Foster's "My Old Kentucky Home" in continual performance poured down from loudspeakers in the crowns of trees. That cooled the story project right off the bat, the fact notwithstanding that Heaven Hill, of Bardstown, Kentucky, was making Elijah Craig and Fighting Cock. Barton, of Bardstown, was making Tom Moore. Driving on, this is what I also learned: Jim Beam, of Clermont, Kentucky, made Knob Creek, Old Grand-Dad, Booker's, Baker's, Basil Hayden, and I.W. Harper. Brown-Foreman, of Louisville, Kentucky, made Early Times, Old Forester, and Woodford Reserve. Buffalo Trace, of Frankfort, Kentucky, made many other not-well-known brands, including Pappy Van Winkle. Bernheim Distillery, of Louisville, Kentucky, made Rebel Yell. Maker's Mark, of Loretto, Kentucky, made Maker's Mark.

I have been through most of that list—not smashed before a row of jiggers but sober, scientific, and sensitive to the lighter, rather objectionable alcohols (a phrase I picked up from George Harbinson, the managing director and chairman of Macallan, Speyside). A bourbon previously unknown to me was Bulleit, whose label said it was from Louisville and did not mention age. Its website said it was from Lawrenceburg, Kentucky, and was five to eight years old. Lawrenceburg, Kentucky, on the deeply incised Kentucky River, is where Austin Nichols makes Wild Turkey. The view from far above, down at the distillery across the river, is competitive with scenes along the Rhine. Driving around Kentucky looking at distilleries is a good way of getting to know the state, and it beats the hell out of horses.

My closest call ever with the Bing cherry came in 1982, during a touristy drive through northwestern Washington on a route that crossed the Cascade Range and went down into the Okanogan Valley. Trending north through Washington and into British Columbia, the Okanogan Valley is the Oxford and Cambridge of the Bing cherry. Aware of this and caving by the minute, I had learned the name of a widely admired orchard we would pass, owned and farmed by a knowledgeable married couple who will prefer to remain nameless.

This cherry had been bred in 1875 at an orchard in Oregon, on the Willamette River, just south of Portland. In an open-pollination cross, its mother was a Black Republican and its father a Royal Ann (*sic*). The orchard foreman was Ah Bing. A Manchurian well over six feet tall, he spent several decades in the United States, sending home to his wife and children money from his long employment at what had been one of Oregon's pioneer nurseries. Its founder, Henderson Lewelling, brought his fruit trees and his family overland by oxcart from Iowa.

In a memoir written many years after the fact, a member of the family recalled that Ah Bing had under his personal supervision the row of test trees in which the successful cultivar appeared. In any case, he was the foreman and the cherry was named for him. Taxonomy went elsewhere. The Bing cherry, of the species *Prunus avium*, has the medicinal implications of a prune. Ripening, it tends to split if too much rain falls on it. Hence this red cherry, by far the most popular in America, is mainly grown in the dry-summer valleys of Washington, Oregon, and California.

The Chinese Exclusion Act and the Immigration Act of 1882 were passed by the forty-seventh U.S. Congress, alarmed by the great numbers of Chinese laborers who had been drawn to Western farms and orchards, to the construction of railroads, to placer and hard-rock mines. The acts categorized their kind as inadmissible aliens and banned immigration by Chinese laborers for ten years. For those already living in the United States, the path to citizenship was occluded. Ah Bing made his last trip home in 1889.

Full of anticipation, at least on my part, my wife, Yolanda, and I breezed across the North Cascades and descended into the Okanogan Valley. Desiccated. Lovely. Irrigation-green. Trees punctuated with deep red dots. We found the orchard we meant to visit, its barn open, post-and-beam, Bing cherries in hanging baskets, shelved baskets, indoors and out, a broad ramp lined with cherries, some in boxes. Oh, the soft, tart skin, the pulpy, tangy flesh, the prognosticating pits. Out of the car, I started up the ramp, and heard shouting, angry shouting, more shouting, and the married owners appeared, on the apron of their barn, in a fistfight.

Dropped Antaeus

I once owned a small sculpture, on a flat base about seven inches wide, of a prizefighter who had just been decked. Knocked over backward on his ass, he was propped on his elbows looking dazed. The piece was given to me by the sculptor, Joe Brown, whose dual role at Princeton University was professor of art and artist in residence. Joe had also been a prizefighter, a fact to which his nose permanently testified, and he had been the coach of varsity boxing until my father, whose role at Princeton was in sports medicine, killed boxing at the university for what appears to be all time. Joe didn't seem to mind. Sculpture was his vocation. Born in 1909, he died in 1985, and was the creator of four hundred representational works, ranging from the bust of Louis Brandeis at Harvard Law School and the bust of Robert Frost in the Amherst public library to the larger-than-life sculptures of football and baseball players outside the stadium complex in South Philadelphia.

My little prizefighter, made of plaster, had a larger-than-life counterpart. It appeared one day in the entrance hall of Princeton's main library and must have been carried in there by at least eight stevedores. The head was the size of a beach ball, the muscles fantastic. Joe's title for the piece was *Dropped Antaeus*, and Antaeus at five hundred pounds, more or less, seemed to be in even greater need for whatever his mother Earth could do for him than he did in my small version. Joe had a point to make about that. A precise, volumetric change of scale—enlarging, for example, a ten-inch figure into a ten-foot figure—will not succeed in the eye of the beholder. Hands will not only be larger but can seem grotesquely larger. Same for feet, faces, feathers of a bird. With more than a tape measure, the artist has to adjust the art.

The entrance hall of Princeton's main library—Harvey S. Firestone Memorial Library—wasn't there when I was ten years old. The library itself—with its acreages of subterranean floors, its millions of books, its tip-of-the-iceberg schistose tower—wasn't there. A broad and sloping lawn was there, white pines. A small brownstone building was the only structure in that large space, and it stood almost exactly on the site of the entrance hall where the amplified Antaeus would someday drop. This wee brownstone building—a nineteenth-century relic, its original purpose forgotten—was Joe Brown's sculpture studio. He taught students there, and did his own work there when he was not at the gym with his boxers. The place was full of modelling clay, and always full of human figures evolving in clay and supported on backirons. Much of the day, no one was there.

The brownstone was locked when no one was there, but one of my fifth-grade friends discovered that if you climbed a wall to a single-pane double-hung window, you could lift the lower half of the window and cross the sill. He went home with a few pounds of clay. He gave me some. I gave some of that to my brother, six years older, a junior at Princeton High School. This is the moment when my brother enters the assembling facts not only as an indictable accomplice but as the spontaneous mastermind—the El Capo—of a clay-stealing cartel consisting of himself and four ten-year-olds. I had no interest in modelling clay. He did. He sat at his desk making figurines, and I was out back shooting baskets. He was my older brother, though, source of guidance and wisdom. The least I could do was do as I was told, and steal the college clay for him. I went up the brownstone wall and lifted the window twice more.

The figures close to completion were women, for the most part. Venus. Minerva. Bits of extraneous clay were all over their bodies for reasons I could not imagine. Certain participant ten-year-olds rolled clay between their palms making cylinders a couple of inches long, which they added as penises to Venus and Minerva. Extraneous clay.

On the final visit, I was the first to leave. Feet-first, sliding backward on my belly, I went over the windowsill. My legs moved down, my feet hunting for purchase in the wall. A hand grabbed one of my ankles and held on like a leg iron. "Got you," said Francis X. Hogarty, a university proctor. "I tracked your feet in the snow."

My father wasn't much interested in the immediate fate of the other ten-year-olds, but he made up for it in the concentration of his attention to me. If he said anything to El Capo, I was not aware of it. What is most indelible in my memory is that he told me to get into the car and we drove to Joe Brown's on Edwards Place. Faculty housing. Row housing. Gwyneth King in the parlor with Joe. No one called her Mrs. Brown. She wouldn't hear of it. How difficult a position for Joe to be in. The director of athletic medicine had come to him with a ten-year-old perp in a crime of which Joe was the victim. Joe and the university. Within moments of our arrival, Joe grasped the situation, its implications and ramifications. I don't remember what he said, but—it seems miraculous—his reactions and comments assuaged rather than crushed me, and simultaneously pacified my humiliated father. I went home guilty as charged, but with a relieved sense that I would make it to the sixth grade. No need to add that I would revere Joe Brown forever.

In 1965, he did a sculptural likeness of Bill Bradley, a Princeton senior who won a gold medal in basketball at the 1964 Olympics. The piece is listed among Joe's statuettes, with other Olympians, like track-and-field's Jesse Owens (1936) and the swimmer Duke Kahanamoku (1912, 1920). Bradley—crouched, head up, butt out, looking especially athletic—holds a basketball in both hands and off his right side, protecting it. You can feel the defense to his left. I can, anyway. I am looking at the statuette as I write. Joe gave me this plaster original in that same year, when my first book was published and its subject was Bill Bradley.

At some point back there, about a dozen years after my own graduation, I was visiting Joe in his new studio, in the new architecture building, and he was flattening bits of clay between thumb and forefinger, then applying them to the surface of a statue that to me looked perfectly proportioned, smooth, and finished. Venus? Minerva? No. But shout, memory. Joe, what are you doing? You are messing up a beautiful piece of work right near the finish.

Yes. Not to any great extent, though. When you are close like this, nearing satisfaction on something that has taken a very long time to do, you don't want to be tempted to decide too soon that you are done. You need to add time for a final assessment of the overall form and structure before removing these bits of clay and polishing the detail.

In the effects of a change of scale (the enlarging of Antaeus), there is an artistic message that carries beyond sculpture and into other realms, like writing, and I'm still trying to figure out how best to summarize it, relating, as it does, to the idea that a piece of writing ought not to be planned for a given size but developed to the length most suitable to the material, and no farther.

Meanwhile, there is nothing ambiguous about those flattened-on-the-forefinger bits of clay.

Generation P

We process grief. We process failure. We process trauma. We process cheese. We are Generation P, the word processors. Thinking through is not what we do. We have wrapped our heads around the most amazing things. Quantum mechanics. Orgo.

How did it go?

Crushed it.

Can you crush the electoral college?

Still working on it, thinking outside the box.

The ballot box?

Yes, meme. Never merely active, we are prefixed proactive. A damn? We don't give it. We pivot.

What is your icon?

A suitcase. It's full of assertions, instructions, amendments, concepts, and ideas. We unpack all that. Then we wrap our heads around it. The pushback is not impactful.

And will you be doing so in the future?

Let me walk you through it, going forward. As said on NPR: "We're interested in what's going to happen going forward."

What do you normally do when you are expected to inform, notify, apprise, indicate, point out, show, or tell?

We share. From kindergarten going forward we will never forget it. Get this. NPR: "The Utah highway department shared photos of the monolith."

Wow.

To negotiate with us, just come to the table. We have your back. We take it to the next level.

Wow.

It's a takeaway!

Wowee!

The Monks of Pharma

Some of my favorite authors work in what I imagine to be dark little ill-painted cells in the halls of big pharma. I don't know any of them, but they populate my imagination, and they are real. More than real, they are neologymnasts. Annually, they coin more words than the Sumerians did in three thousand years. I was made aware of their existence by my retired friend George Hackl, of central New Hampshire, who travelled the world for E. R. Squibb & Sons (now Bristol Myers Squibb), licensing foreign companies to sell patented Squibb drugs, and, conversely, Squibb to sell the drugs of English, Spanish, French, Italian, German, Swiss, Polish, Latvian, Israeli, Japanese, and Australian companies, among others. He once imparted to me the sly commercial purpose—underlying all official requirements and functions—of generic names.

The patent on a drug lasts twenty years. After that—as everyone has come to know—the patentee continues to make the drug and sell it under its brand (or trade) name, but any other company is now free to make the same drug and sell it under its generic name. So when the originating company coins the brand and generic names, it tries to make the brand name attractive but the generic name a polysyllabic nightmare. George said this was not something done by just anybody, by your average authorial hack. It was done by a category of wordsmiths for centuries unknown outside monasteries. In a daydream, I observed them deep in a basement of big pharma under the inspiring leadership of the Dalai Logo, or senior manager of trademark development. The monks of pharma know from logarithms. They can throw an extra syllable that can stop a train.

Oddly, all this has reminded me of writers in their cubicles at *The New Yorker*. It reminds me of a description of them written long ago by my revered colleague Brendan Gill (1914–1997):

> A friend of mine, Patrick Kavanagh, who was the premier poet in Ireland after Yeats, said of the peasantry from which he sprang that they live in the dark cave of the unconscious and they scream when they see the light. They *scream* when they see the light. Now, most *New Yorker* writers share this attribute with Irish peasants. They tend to be lonely, mole-like creatures, who work in their own portable if not peasant darkness and who seldom utter a sound above a groan. It happens that I am not like that. On the contrary, I am among those who enjoy the light and even, to a certain extent, the limelight . . .
>
> In the offices of *The New Yorker* is a long corridor off which . . . a couple of dozen . . . writers and editors have their bleak little ill-painted cells. The silence in that corridor is so profound and continuous that [one of them] long ago christened it Sleepy Hollow.

Yes, and when the writers woke up, they were expected to be at least half as creative as the monks of pharma, a need that tended to bring on more sleep. It was a monk of pharma who coined ibuprofen, probably not the same one who called it Advil. And all the confreres are completely at home with every class of drug from the ergoloid mesylates to the macrolide antibiotics. They know the difference between Elavil and amitriptyline—none—even if the words were made in someone else's basement. From acamprosate (Campral) to zonisamide (Zonegran), their conjurations begin with twenty-one initial letters, never with h, j, k, w, or y, because those letters don't exist in some languages.

At twenty-eight-hundred dollars a pop, Olumiant is obviously the sort of drug that wants an unfathomable, unmemorizable, twenty-eight-hundred-dollar generic shadow. It has one (baricitinib).

Lyrica (pregabalin)
Casodex (bicalutamide)
Evista (raloxifene)
Tylenol (acetaminophen)
Flomax (tamsulosin)
Veklury (remdesivir)
Remicade (infliximab)
Yasmin (drospirenone)
Xanax (alprazolam)
Accolate (zafirlukast)

In order to be sure that a new word like, say, umeclidinium is not dirty or blasphemous anywhere in the world, the monks need to know at least six thousand languages. Of them, the youngest and fastest-growing is their own Linguapharma.

O Beautiful for Stripes and Stars

How long does it take to sing "The Star-Spangled Banner"?

Roughly one minute and four seconds.

How long does it take a spangled sport singer to sing "The Star-Spangled Banner"?

Six and a half hours. Or so it seems.

The first verse, the only one most of us ever hear, asks two questions: Is our country still here? And will it be here through the long future?

Question 3: How long does it take to ask two questions?

"The Star-Spangled Banner" is a melody of a hundred and six beats that take sixty-four seconds to play, so the average beat is held about three-fifths of a second—or "one Missis . . ."—a liberal amount but not nearly enough if you want to spangle with the stars. In that case, your words need to expand into the four-second range, and your self-absorption needs to be quasi-total while your ululations become ulululations and your ulululations become ulululululations and your ulululululations become ululululululations. Any athlete standing up and listening would do well to get down on one knee and rest.

The time that will be taken to sing the national anthem at the next Super Bowl has been an object of online prop betting for many years. Bettors choose over or under a prop like one minute and fifty-nine seconds. Alicia Keys set the record in 2013 at two minutes and thirty-five seconds.

Musicologically, the anthem is not without inherent flaws. The music fails to match the questions the lyrics are asking. The notes descend where they should rise. When things are gallantly streaming and when our flag was still there, a question is being asked, but in the music there is no interrogative uplift, no ascending arpeggio. Instead, the notes somberly go downstairs, asking nothing. This could be fixed by reversing two words. Change "Oh, say, can you see?" to "Oh, say, you can see." Delete the question mark.

"America the Beautiful" has been sung concomitantly at Super Bowls, e.g. 2020 and 2021, when it seemed, in length, to be up there with "The Star-Spangled Banner." "America the Beautiful" was written in 1893 as a thirty-two-line, four-stanza poem by Katharine Lee Bates, a thirty-four-year-old professor of English literature from Wellesley College, after summiting Pikes Peak, exhausted on a mule. Her imagery is sometimes as beautiful as the view that inspired it, at other times as purple as the mountain itself—here a fine image followed by a bad one followed by a fine one followed by a bad one, bringing on nose wrinkles and pallesthesia in more or less equal proportion. Its articles and pronouns have a King James religiosity that suggests a priestly government and has failed to accompany this old sports fan into the twenty-first century, its cities dimmed by human tears. And what does she mean by spacious skies? Is the sky any less spacious over New Jersey than it is over Scotland? Is the distance to the sun notably greater in Bozeman than in Boston? Will Montana ever realize that from human perspective the biggest sky is in a place like Amarillo, where the ground is flat to all horizons? This is a losing battle. Walker Percy described the sky above Chicago as naked and lonely. "America the Beautiful" is sung to the music of an earlier hymn, by Samuel A. Ward (1848–1903). Herewith four revised verses:

O beautiful for spacious skies,
For amber waves of grain,
For purple mountain majesties
Above the fruited plain!
America! America!
God shed His grace on thee
And crown thy good with
    brotherhood
From sea to shining sea!

O beautiful for pilgrim feet
Whose stern impassioned stress
A thoroughfare of freedom
    beat
Across the wilderness!
America! America!
God mend thine every flaw,
Confirm thy soul in self-control,
Thy liberty in law!

O beautiful for heroes proved
In liberating strife,
Who more than self their
    country loved
And mercy more than life!
America! America!
May God thy gold refine
Till all success be nobleness
And every gain divine!

O beautiful for azure skies,
For amber waves of grain,
For purple mountains rising high
Above the fruited plain.
America, America,
Beware the doctrinaire
And crown your good with
    brotherhood,
Your systems ever fair.

O beautiful for pioneers
Whose stern impassioned stress
A thoroughfare of freedom
    beat
Across the wilderness.
America, America,
Amend your every flaw,
Confirm your soul in self-control,
Your liberty in law.

O beautiful for heroes proved
In liberating strife.
Who more than self their
    country loved
And justice more than life.
America, America,
Go forward on that line
Till all success be nobleness
And every gain combine.

O beautiful for patriot dream	O beautiful for patriot dream
That sees beyond the years	That sees beyond the years,
Thine alabaster cities gleam	Where alabaster cities gleam
Undimmed by human tears!	Undimmed by human tears.
America! America!	America, America,
God shed His grace on thee	Beware the doctrinaire
And crown thy good with	And crown your good with
brotherhood	brotherhood,
From sea to shining sea!	Your systems ever fair.

Highlander

In a box on a shelf among some old unvisited books, I came upon three rock specimens and a motor yacht. I couldn't remember how I had acquired or why I had kept those particular rocks. A labelled tremolite from Sparta, New Jersey? And I was even more mystified by the motor yacht—a toy, a paperweight, five and a half inches long, heavier than stone. I showed it to my wife, Yolanda, who can see better than I can, and she found its name in tiny white type on a black stripe amidships: The Highlander.

Oh, my. Malcolm Forbes. His yacht. A party favor. Party of a-hundred-and-thirty-odd on the yacht to watch the Fourth of July fireworks in the East River. Mick Jagger. People like that. People from all over the news, the media, the world, the city. Lobsters. Smoked salmon. Caviar by the kilo. What Yolanda and I were doing there remains unclear, but it may have had something to do with Rhodes Scholarship applications in 1979. A senior from my writing class at Princeton University was applying then, and he asked me to write to the Rhodes selection committee a letter recommending him. In a two-stage process in those years, winners were chosen regionally and then nationally. And if, for example, you were a Princeton student and came from Minnesota, you had your choice of applying to the committee in Minnesota or the committee in New Jersey. This kid had limited options because New Jersey was his home state. An appealing and engaging person, he was a fine student, a good writer, an accomplished athlete—the exact profile laid down by Cecil Rhodes. My letter wasn't short. Computers were in the future then, and I can't remember what I said.

The chair of New Jersey's Rhodes Scholarship Selection Committee was Bruce McClellan, head of the Lawrenceville School and a Rhodes scholar himself. I knew him well because we played tennis together. There were no attachments to e-mail then—in fact, no e-mail—and all recommendation letters were photocopied and distributed to the members of the committee, one of whom was Malcolm Forbes, who printed my recommendation letter in *Forbes* magazine, of which he was the owner and the editor. When I learned of this and told Bruce McClellan, his words could have scuttled The Highlander.

Son of the magazine's founder, Forbes was a 1941 Princeton graduate, a decorated machine gunner in France, a motorcycle fanatic who gave a Purple Passion Harley-Davidson to his friend Elizabeth Taylor. He led a motorcycle gang called the Capitalist Tools. Bertie Charles Forbes, his father, was a Scot born in Aberdeenshire, whose journalistic experience began in Dundee. None of that is in the Highlands, but let that go. His mother's name was Agnes. When Malcolm graduated from Princeton, I was ten years old. I was essentially unaware of his existence until an event at Princeton Junction in the nineteen-sixties. I was up on the platform as a train was pulling in, bound for New York. A car—a Jeep, if memory serves—came lickety-split into view, obviously containing someone late for the train. It went for the closest parking lot. The entrance and exit were side by side. The entrance had a boom barrier and ways of getting paid, the exit was defended by a row of spikes, angled toward the tires of any car that might try to enter the lot the wrong way. Malcolm Forbes was in the Jeep, as I was soon to learn. He didn't live in Princeton. He lived in Far Hills. He just hung around Princeton long enough to give it an undergraduate college. He didn't have a card that would raise a boom barrier at Princeton Junction. As the New York train was squealing to a stop, he drove his Jeep right over the spikes in an attempt to enter the exit. Pop. Pow. Hiss. Bam. Who is that? On the platform, more than one person knew the answer.

Twenty years later, I was present at the dedication of Forbes College, named for Malcolm's son Steve. Malcolm spoke with ebullience, and I wish I could quote him exactly, but his topic sentence was essentially this: "Anyone who tells you money can't buy happiness is crazy."

The happiness he was buying that Fourth of July night on The Highlander began at a pier in the Hudson River. The yacht was a hundred and fifty feet long, with promenades, staterooms, mirrored salons, and two lifeboats. A Gainsborough in a salon, a Cocteau in another. Dufy. There were quasi-nautical memorabilia, like stained glass off a royal yacht, panels in Art Deco from the

Normandie, and everywhere over everything the deep blue setts of the Forbes tartan. The lobsters may have arrived in an eighteen-wheeler. The wine. We went slowly down the western shore of Manhattan and turned left in the bay. Darkness was falling and the lights of the city grew bright. On barges in the East River, south of the Brooklyn Bridge, specialists were prepared to set off pyrotechnical novelties. This was the focal point of an all but un-ending vastness of fireworks, millions of people massed for the view, crowds incredibly deep on the Lower East Side. Softly, The Highlander approached the Lower East Side, cut its power, and came to a stop at the Manhattan seawall, where it blocked the view of a hundred and fifty feet of crowd as we watched the Roman candles.

La Torre Pendente

In 1962, when I was working for *Time: The Weekly Newsmagazine* and doing freelance pieces to help pay for the construction of our house, I got into a piece on the stability of towers like the leaning one in Pisa. Reading about them, I of course made notes, which came to nothing published and spent the next six decades in a base-ment filing cabinet covered with mole crickets. The notes were also covered with puns, enough to make anybody crawl off in shame.

Notes:

Already seventeen feet out of plumb, the tower is leaning more each year and, while there is much disagreement on the actual date of the toppling, Italian engineers seem to take it for granted that if something is not done their Torre Pendente will one day come down in a spectacular shower of tourists and white marble. Some say the tower will fall by the turn of the 21st century, others that it is good for at least another three hundred years. Whenever someone with an appropriate title—Professor of Geodesy and Topography, University of Rome; Professor of Architecture, University of Pisa—wants to cry timber for the leaning tower, he can be sure that his words will reverberate through the presses of several continents. In 1950, for example, a subheadline on a Leaning Tower story in *The New York Times* said "Fall Expected Within 50 Years," and below was an alarming reminder that the now-reconstructed campanile in Venice's Piazza San Marco crashed without warning in 1902. Three years ago, a professor at the University of Milan, understandably keyed up because he is a native of Pisa, wondered if the tower were "rushing toward catastrophe; if we keep in mind such things as earthquakes like the one in 1846, the collapse might come at any moment." Then other news items are required to straighten the facts if not the building. They are full of reassurances, almost always from Pisa. Ranieri Niccioli, who has been called the "doctor of il campanile," adopts a detached, slightly disgusted tone about the ex-Pisan at the University of Milan. "I understand Professor Pecchai is a man of letters," he says. A lawyer named Giuseppe Ramalli, administrator of the Pisan cathedral group, tells a nationwide radio audience: "We are very happy for the interest manifested in continuous and anxious appeals that come from all parts of the earth, but we do not desire an unjustified alarm. The tower of our town is the object of most careful attention." A hundred and fifty thousand tourists a season must not be given the wrong slant.

. . . as late as 1900, a majority of the world's architectural historians held the view that the tower had been purposely constructed on an angle as a tourist attraction, and strong controversy on the point had eventually ended in favor of those who held that just as Shakespeare wrote his own plays the tower followed its own inclinations . . . the lean is not the building's only abnormality; it has curvature of the spine.

Begun August 9, 1173, the campanile in the Piazza del Duomo at Pisa showed an affinity for the horizontal almost at once. One trouble was that while Bonanno Pisano, the architect, had adequate capabilities above the ground, he was born with no talent beneath the surface. To support an eight-story marble tower that would weigh some sixteen thousand tons, he built a foundation not more than ten feet deep and no greater in diameter than the structure above—and all on the porous alluvial soil of the Arno delta.

Modern engineers have said that the tower's weight per square centimeter at ground level is about five times the maximum for that sort of ground, something Bonanno had discovered empirically. After three stories were built, the tower leaned so rakishly that work was stopped. Like the Washington Monument, it stood half finished for years, embarrassing local citizens.

In Pisa, there was particular cause for dissatisfaction. During the 12th century, a fondness for campaniles had spread through northern Italy—Bologna built two, the ill-fated bell tower in Venice's Piazza San Marco was completed in 1156—but Pisa in Tuscany had only a sloping fragment. Tilt or no tilt, the city needed a full-grown, singing tower.

Against the special handicap, new architects struggled, but the building process went on intermittently for two centuries. Bonanno had already begun to compensate for the lean by adding something extra on the low side of each story—perhaps unconsciously, since his masons would automatically have finished them off at ninety degrees to the perpendicular, and the variation between the high and low sides is only fourteen centimeters up to the fourth story, where Bonanno quit. After that, the curvature of the tower increases sharply. The fifth, sixth, and seventh stories, variously credited to Giovanni di Simone, Benenato Bottici, and William of Innsbruck, show a difference of thirty-four centimeters, giving the tower the appearance of a heavy woman with protruding buttocks.

The belfry, built up thirty-eight centimeters on the low side, tilts like a head cocked for listening and gives the tower a total variance, from one side to the other, of eighty-six centimeters, or thirty-four inches. The belfry's architect is unknown, but was probably Tommaso di Andrea da Pontedera, son of the sculptor Andrea Pisano. The tower was completed—about a hundred and eighty-five feet high and fifty-one feet in diameter—in the latter half of the 14th century.

If the campanile then began to serve the town, it had to wait two centuries to serve the world. Professor Galileo Galilei had not yet resigned from the faculty of the University of Pisa when he climbed the tower and dropped the unequal weights that added, in colleagues' eyes, an unwelcome shock of truth to his already unpopular and unorthodox points of view. The weights fell with equal velocity and Galileo didn't last long at Pisa, but he had dropped onto its unsteady soil the first principles of dynamics. This much-told story of Galileo and the tower is apocryphal.

As the next three and a half centuries passed and the leaning tower continued its flight from plumb, it brought visitors in multiplying numbers and—all because the original architect had been a failure as an engineer—became one of Europe's treasured landmarks.

Efforts have been made to arrest the lean, but not with total success. In the early nineteen-thirties, some nine hundred tons of concrete were poured into three hundred and sixty-one holes around the tower's base and the "shifty shaft," as one writer has irreverently called it, held still. During wartime fighting in the Arno Valley, a shell nicked it with no serious results, but three bombs fell nearby and their effect may have been more telling. At any rate, soon after the Second World War—and soon after a damaging flood—measurements showed that the Leaning Tower of Pisa was actively leaning again.

Pisa has not had to seek advice about the tower's salvation. It has come freely from many quarters, none less practical than the Milan literary professor who wondered if engineers couldn't somehow lift the campanile and hold it in the air while workmen strengthened the foundation beneath. Unobtrusively, the building has been loaded with iron supports, braces, and counterweights. Of the seven bells in the upper story, the heaviest—three and a half tons—is hung prudently on the high side, and since 1934 the bells have been tolled with clapper ropes to avoid swinging them on their axles. Two seismographs monitor earth disturbances, and heavy traffic is kept away; but a surveyors' theodolite has been installed and the angles it records keep changing for the worse.

The late Charles B. Spencer, who was president of a New York engineering firm that specializes in underpinning, thought the lean could be corrected in one of four ways. On the low side, the tower could be given a horizontal push, or something could be added to the foundation. On the high side, the foundation could be whittled down, or a horizontal pull could be applied. The latter expedient was attempted somewhat unprofessionally on New Year's Day, 1959, when a car full of schnoggered tourists, whose nationality was never determined, backed up to the tower, ran a cable from the base to the bumper of their car, and pulled away. The torre remained pendente, but the bumper ripped off and clattered on the pavement.

Electro-petrification is the specialty of a Polish engineer named Romuald Cebertowicz, and he would like to use it to save the leaning tower. He injects silica gel into the soil, then applies a strong electrical field that causes the gel particles to spread evenly, then harden. A University of Rome professor thinks the only sound remedy is to dismantle the tower slab by slab and rebuild it on a huge, new foundation. But what the tower's potential saviors don't seem to comprehend is that most Pisans would not like to see their tower fixed. There is emotional capital in its precariousness. A rebuilt leaning tower would be only slightly more authentic than the Parthenon in Nashville or the Leaning Tower of Chicago. (A rich Chicagoan once reproduced Pisa's tower in his back yard.)

There is an essential mystery about the Leaning Tower of Pisa and its half-cocked demeanor. Animals have been known to walk the long way around it and, if taken inside, quiver and want to get away. People climb its two hundred and ninety-three steps with no concern, drink aperitifs in its shadow, and pay millions of lire a year in homage to it. Upright but slightly ajar, the tower has plenty in common with humanity, and may, if its catastrophe comes as predicted, share the same fate.

Disaster has happened before in Pisa. When the tower was

begun, the city was a healthy seaport, rich and growing richer. In the thirteenth century, the Arno abruptly changed its course. Where there had been a harbor, mud flats remained. The city, now seven miles from the sea, atrophied to little more than an over-built village, and was forced to wait until the era of the money-spending tourist for a new source of capital from abroad. Tourists, of course, admire the entire cathedral group—the cathedral, the baptistery, the leaning campanile, and the Campo Santo burial ground, whose frescoes and statuary were half destroyed by war—all in the ornate, detailed, repetitively arcaded stile Pisano, the special architectural characteristic of that part of Tuscany. But they come to see the tower. "What a pity for Pisa," a Roman cardinal once said, "if its tower ever collapsed or stood up straight."

Grateful Pisans now call their Piazza del Duomo the "piazza of miracles," because they think it is a miracle that so much useful Romanesque beauty could have been created in one place. The tower's saucy tilt, some say, is the unexpected stroke that trans-forms the square into a composite work of art. Their concern is no less genuine for its lack of anxiety. They have no need to be anx-ious, anyway, according to one apocryphal legend, which claims that the tower rests comfortably against the prevailing winds. With the wind as a cradle, it cannot fall.

———————

In the six decades since those notes were written, the torre pendente has not been unattended. For a time in the nineteen-nineties, huge slabs of lead, collectively weighing nearly a thou-sand tons, were placed against the high side. Seventy-seven tons of soil were removed from under the high side. The remedial effort between 1993 and 2001 reduced the tower's tilt from 5.5 to 3.97 degrees. The earth itself is tilting 23.5 degrees so why not a tower in Italy? Students of Pisan history think that Diotisalvi was the first architect in the two centuries of construction. Whatever knowledge of foundation engineering he and others may have lacked, it is ironic that the spongy texture of Pisan soil may have saved the tower from complete destruction by earthquake—at least four major temblors having occurred in the region since the thirteenth century. As global warming rolls on past the present, the tower will be ever more vulnerable to a catastrophe that was unimaginable through its first eight centuries. Its base is seven feet above sea level.

————————

And finally, with those sixty-year-old notes I found an addendum I didn't recognize:

The word for schadenfreude in Spanish is schadenfreude. An example of the genre—titled "La Torre Inclinada Pisana"—tells its story with a distinctly Spanish perspective, as when the author is savoring a list of the bell towers in Italy that have toppled like duckpins through time.

> Un campanario en la Plaza San Marcos de Venecia se cayó
>   estrepitosamente—puf—nel año 1902.
> Un campanario en Orvieto en el siglo XIV—puf!
> Un campanario en Ferrara en el siglo XV—puf!
> En Palermo en el siglo XVI—puf!
> En Mantua en el siglo XVII—puf!
> En Padua en el siglo XVIII—puf!

La ciudad de Bologna tiene dos torres inclinadas del siglo
doce que no han caído todavía. Vamos a ver.

Extended study of this acid document has yielded the recollection that the author was me—*sí, yo mismo*—for a Spanish class at
the Princeton Adult School fifty years ago. Puf!

Beantown

In 1947, I spent the summer in Wisconsin, caddying at a golf course
called Tuscumbia. I was staying with a family in Ripon, twelve
miles away, and I hitchhiked to the golf club each morning. The
family were the Hettingers, who had moved back to Ripon from
Princeton, New Jersey, where Leonard Hettinger had worked in
the university's Department of Athletics during the Second World
War and had coached the 1944–45 basketball team. Departing
at the end of 1945, the Hettingers left their son, Mike, with our
family, to finish his sophomore year (and mine) at Princeton High
School. We both played basketball there and paid close attention
to little else. That summer, Mike went back to Ripon. And I followed, in reciprocity, a year later.

Riding north into Wisconsin from Chicago in a train with its
windows open, and drawing in the aroma of new-mown hay, I
thought I was going to be working in a pea cannery, where Mike
had a job, but it turned out that the cannery did not have enough
jobs even for local kids, so I ended up in the company of the
caddies at Tuscumbia. It would not be a gross exaggeration to call

them surly. They sat around the caddy shack waiting to be called onto the course, and they eyed me with no warmth. After several days, they got up some curiosity, and one of them said, "Where do you come from, kid?"

I'll admit I was cock proud that I had been born in a municipal Valhalla that had within it an academic Xanadu, its Gothic spires the topless towers of Ilium, its storm drains running over with beer. I was sixteen years old. Where did I come from, kid? With all the self-awareness of a golf ball, I drew myself up and responded in a voice meant to suggest the Magna Carta. Slowing the syllables, I said the magic word, "Princeton."

In a tone of utmost superiority, the boy who had asked the question said, "Oh. Beantown."

Princeton, Wisconsin, unknown to me and nine miles away in a direction opposite Ripon, obviously held no prestige in the caddy shack and seemed to be known for its beans. As further dialogue revealed, the caddies had no more respect for Ripon than they had for Beantown, the facts notwithstanding that Ripon had a liberal-arts college (1851) and Ripon was where the Republican Party was founded (1854). I was as awestruck by their provincialism as I was unaware of my own.

If I had been caddying in the Sierra Nevada near a town that was once called Princeton, would my origins have suffered such scorn? Most unlikely. Californians of every ilk know what's in them thar hills, know that the very sound of the Princeton name suggests capital gain, endowment wallows, and envy of Harvard. They actually changed the name long ago from Princeton to Mount Bullion. Never mind that Senator Thomas Hart Benton was called Old Bullion and they thought they were naming it for him—at a time, as it happens, when the school now outside my office window was known as the College of New Jersey. Founded in 1746, it was a hundred and fifty years old when it changed its name.

I once thought of writing a piece about Princetons other than Princeton but fought off the idea as the journalistic equivalent of revisiting events on their anniversaries, of wilderness camping by Jeep Cherokee, of psychoanalyzing the Mummers Parade. There are Princetons in fully half the states of the United States, including several ghost towns. All the extant ones are small—most with populations in four and three (!) digits—and the largest (Princeton, Florida) is about thirty-six thousand, five thousand more than Princeton, New Jersey. Nearly all are named for people named Prince or for scattered mines named Princeton Mine for more people named Prince. So much for the topless towers.

Princeton, Montana, at the junction of Princeton Gulch and Boulder Creek Canyon, eighty-four miles southwest of Helena, sixty-nine miles northwest of Butte, is a ghost town, its school, its hotel, most of its houses gone. From 1882 onward, the Princeton Mining Company worked the lode—silver, gold, lead, phosphate—until there was no more silver, gold, lead, or phosphate. There are two Princetons in eastern Texas, one a ghost town. A second Princeton, California—on the Sacramento River near Yuba City—lives on (pop. 337).

Princeton, Florida, was named by Gaston Drake, of the Princeton Class of 1894, and is the only Princeton named for the university. Some of its buildings were painted orange and black, the school's colors. It is on the Florida East Coast Railway in Miami-Dade County, where Drake sawed and sold lumber until 1923, when there were no more trees. The town's population is half white, half Hispanic/Latino.

Princeton, Idaho, was named in 1894 by a settler from Princeton, Minnesota. Princeton, Kansas, was named for Princeton, Illinois. Princeton, Maine, was named for Princeton, Massachusetts. Princeton, Minnesota, named in 1856 for John S. Prince, is fifty miles north of Minneapolis on the Rum River. John S. Prince was either the most revered or the most aggressive of the five people who platted the town. Princeton, Indiana, near the Ohio River, was named in 1814 for William Prince, a county commissioner who immigrated from Ireland when he was forty-two years old. Princeton, Kentucky, was named for a Virginia-born William Prince, who built his Kentucky home above a big spring called Big Spring, which flowed, as it flows today, from a downtown cave. Princeton College, in Princeton, Kentucky, was founded in 1860. Confederate soldiers camped on its campus in 1861, Union soldiers thereafter. It is now a campus of the University of Kentucky, College of Agriculture. Princeton, Massachusetts, north of Worcester, was named in 1759 for Thomas Prince, the author of *A Chronological History of New-England in the Form of Annals* and the pastor of Old South Church in Boston. On Princeton's eastern border is Mount Wachusett, a hyperlink to Henry David Thoreau.

Princeton, Missouri, seat of Mercer County, about halfway between Kansas City and Des Moines, Iowa, was named in 1846 to commemorate the 1777 Battle of Princeton in the American Revolution. The Battle of Princeton occurred on what is now Mercer Street, in Princeton, Mercer County, New Jersey. Hugh Mercer—a Scottish-born, Scotland-trained surgeon in George Washington's Continental Army—died in the battle. Washington's victory sent the redcoats not only out of Princeton but also

out of New Jersey. In 1852, Martha Jane Canary was born in
Princeton, Missouri. In the eighteen-seventies—in Deadwood,
Dakota Territory—she hung out with the likes of Valentine
McGillycuddy and Wild Bill Hickok, and was known as Calam-
ity Jane.

Princeton, West Virginia, is the county seat of Mercer County.

Princeton, New Jersey—surrounded by communities called
Queenston, Kingston, and Princessville—was named in honor
of the Prince of Nassau, Prince of Orange, who became King
William III (1650–1702), benefactor, with his wife, of the College
of William and Mary, and the reason why Princeton University's
oldest and most focal building, which once housed the entire college and the Continental Congress with it, is called Nassau Hall.
Nassau Street is the town's main street. Beantown.

Deep Insight

In 1974, Larry L. King was the entire journalism program at
Princeton, which was not called journalism then but Humanistic
Studies. This was not Larry King the television interviewer in the
antique suspenders. This was the Texan Larry Leo King, who had
published *Confessions of a White Racist* in 1971, and while teaching
at Princeton wrote a piece in *Playboy* that would evolve into the
Broadway musical *The Best Little Whorehouse in Texas*. He was a
self-guided teacher who held office hours with students in a local
barroom. He had signed on to teach four consecutive semesters.
As the third one was nearing its end—in December, 1974—he
evidently decided that he had made a mistake. On New Year's

Day, he would turn forty-six. As a working journalist, he was increasingly inconvenienced by the burdens of teaching. Just before Christmas, he imploded, and quit.

When Larry King quit, his employers, Princeton's Council of the Humanities, were thrown into a deep humanistic swivet. Universities do most things at least a year and a half in advance. They don't sign teachers to begin teaching the week after they sign. Larry King's spring-semester course—Humanistic Studies 440, "The Literature of Fact"—was set to begin on the first day of the new semester. The phone rang in my rented workspace, across Nassau Street from the campus. It was Edward Sullivan, a professor of French and also chair of the Council. Would I fill in for Larry King?

"Yes," I blurted, surprising myself. Not many years earlier, I would never have considered an ancillary commitment, let alone reacted with a spontaneous yes. I was forty-three. At *Time* and *The New Yorker*, I had been writing one piece after another without letup for seventeen years, and may have been feeling a little worn at the edges. I had hoped from college onward to become a staff writer at *The New Yorker* but that had not happened until I was thirty-three, and in the immediate years that followed there was no way that I was going to divert myself from writing *New Yorker* pieces. When I was forty-three, the quick yes emerging from the subconscious had nothing to do with money. *The New Yorker* paid better than Princeton did. A staff writer was paid for words by the bushel, like a farmer, and not by salary, but (extrapolating from the previous decade) I would earn less as a teacher than by spending the same time writing.

So, driven only by some sort of instinct, I filled in for Larry

King. And in a sense I am still filling in for Larry King. I just never left. I remind myself of Mr. Vishniak, who was the Russian expert at *Time* when I worked there in the nineteen-fifties. When the day came for Mr. Vishniak's mandatory retirement, they gave him a watch and a farewell party on the twenty-fifth floor. Mr. Vishniak was grace itself, appreciative, admiring of the watch, accepting many toasts. And on Monday morning, Mr. Vishniak showed up at ten and sat down at his desk. After a couple of years with the Council of the Humanities, I worked out a plan with Professor Sullivan whereby, as time rolled along, I would teach two spring semesters out of three. For practical purposes, this meant that I would teach during six of each thirty-six months. An academic grandfather, I've been doing that for nearly fifty years, floating on a program that has grown and grown.

In the teaching semesters, I wrote nothing of my own. It was like crop rotation. I was fallow. And I was doing something complementary with my own writing—talking about writing with young writers about their writing. I had no way to measure this, but across the years I had the distinct feeling that the refreshment of the teaching months resulted in more writing done by me than I would have done without the teaching.

In 1964, when Princeton began experimenting with courses in journalism, they hired Irving Dilliard, a retired editorial writer for the *St. Louis Post-Dispatch*, who taught alone, spring and fall, and toward the end of his years here was assisted by Landon Jones, a young Princeton graduate who would move on to Time Inc. and eventually become editor of *People*. Larry King replaced Dilliard, and after my first semester the Council of the Humanities hired Haynes Johnson, of *The Washington Post*, to teach a fall-semester course called "Politics and the Press." Haynes's course and my spring course were the whole bit for a couple of years but then the Council, mainly on the effort of its Executive Director, Carol Rigolot, began to expand the program. My own role in the expansion was zero. I just sat and watched while visiting journalists, here to teach one semester, began accumulating in steadily increasing numbers. There have been as many as ten of them teaching in one year. By 2021, more than two hundred had taught in the program.

They have come to teach at Princeton not only from *The Washington Post*, *The New York Times*, the *Los Angeles Times*, *The Times* of London, the *Chicago Tribune*, *The Boston Globe*, and *USA Today*, but also from the Hong Kong *Standard*, the Palestinian Institute for Media Studies, and the South African Broadcasting Corporation. They have come from CNN, ABC, NBC, and NPR. They have come from the Internet and its colony the Blogosphere. From *Sports Illustrated*, *Time*, *Newsweek*, *New York*, and *The New Yorker*. *Rolling Stone*. They have included a producer, several biographers, and a freelance cultural critic. A medical doctor. A documentary filmmaker. Ten alumni have returned to Princeton to teach journalism courses in which they once were students. In 2016, under the long-term appointment of the *Washington Post* investigative reporter Joe Stephens and the Council's current Executive Director, Kathleen Crown, the program was further formalized and acquired a capital P. Soon it was entitled by the university's administration to grant multicourse certificates, sought by students who want to supplement their field of major study with a minor one in journalism.

One of my neighbors and good friends was Edgar Gemmell,

of the Princeton Class of 1934, who returned to the university as an administrator in the nineteen-fifties and before long became a Vice-President. Mainly, he raised money, but he also shepherded funds that came in unsolicited. He told me this story:

In 1964, his office was notified that Edwin Ferris, an alumnus, had perished leaving funds for a professorship in journalism at Princeton. Gemmell before long put in a call to Willard Thorp, the chair of Princeton's English Department, saying, "Willard, I wonder if you would stop in here on your way to the faculty meeting this afternoon. Something has come up." Gemmell's office was in Nassau Hall, the school's oldest and principal building, and so is the Faculty Room. When Thorp showed up, Gemmell told him that the owner and founding editor of *The Scranton Times* had died, and, more recently, the widow of the owner and founding editor of *The Scranton Times* had died, and now the Girard Trust Corn Exchange Bank of Philadelphia had informed the university that ninety-two per cent of the resulting estate had been left to Princeton specifically to establish and maintain a professorship in journalism.

Thorp was a man of exquisite words, each highly selected. He had built a broad critical platform underlying the whole of American literature. He was large of heart and girth. To Gemmell he said, "Over my dead body."

Gemmell looked out the window and up through the canopies of dying elms. Offhandedly, he mentioned that the will said that if Princeton were to refuse the bequest it was to go to the Society of the Home for Friendless Women and Children of the City of Scranton. Then he said, "Willard, the amount of this bequest is . . ."

He named a sum that translates into twenty-first-century money as an attention-getting number of millions of dollars.

Right back, without a flicker, Willard Thorp said, "What this university has long needed is deeper insight into contemporary communications."